اتركوني أَقصُّ لكم
ما رأيتُ...

مقتطفات من **نشيد أوروك**

Let me tell you

what I saw...

Extracts from **Uruk's Anthem**

اتركوني أقصُّ لكم ما رأيتُ...

مقتطفات من *نشيد أوروك*

عدنان الصائغ

تحرير وتقديم: جني لويس

ترجمة: جني لويس وربى أبو غيدا،

وآخرون

دار سيرين للطباعة – كارديف / بريطانيا 2020

Let me tell you what I saw...

Extracts from **Uruk's Anthem**

By Adnan Al-Sayegh

Edited and with an introduction by Jenny Lewis
Translated by Jenny Lewis with Ruba Abughaida
and others

Seren Books, Cardiff / United Kingdom 2020

Seren is the book imprint of
Poetry Wales Press Ltd.
Suite 6, 4 Derwen Road, Bridgend, Wales, CF31 1LH
www.serenbooks.com
facebook.com/SerenBooks
twitter@SerenBooks

The right of Adnan Al-Sayegh to be identified as
the author of this work has been asserted in accordance
with the Copyright, Designs and Patents Act, 1988.

© Adnan Al-Sayegh & Jenny Lewis, 2020.

Introduction © Jenny Lewis 2020.

ISBN: 978-1-78172-602-0
ebook: 978-1-78172-603-7

A CIP record for this title is available from the British Library.

The publisher acknowledges the financial assistance of the Welsh Books Council.

Cover painting by Dr. Ala Bashir (Iraq) by Kind permission of the artist.

Author photograph by Sufyan Al-Khazraji – Stockholm.

Typography by Mouthanna Al-Sayegh.

Printed in Bembo by Pulsioprint.

الفهرست

Contents

تمهيد

نشيدُ أوروك؛ إحدى أطولِ قصائدِ الأدبِ العربيِّ التي كُتِبتْ على الإطلاق، بـ (550) صفحةٍ، تُعبِّرُ عن مدى اليأسِ العميقِ في التجربةِ العراقيةِ. لقد وُصِفتْ بكونها قصيدة جميلة وقوية وشجاعة – وفي الوقتِ نفسِه تستقريءُ برسوخٍ النهاياتِ المروعةَ، وتقاومُ الطغيانَ والديكتاتوريةَ أينما وُجِدا في هذا العالم.

مزجَ نشيدُ أوروك بين التقاليدِ الشعريةِ العربيّةِ والشعرِ السومريِّ القديم، مع العديدِ من السماتِ الإبداعيةِ والتجريبيةِ لكلٍّ من الأدبين: العربي والغربي، لذا يمكنُ وصفُه بشكلٍ أفضل على إنّهُ قصيدة حالمة حداثوية تتصاعدُ في كثيرٍ من الأحيانِ بهيئةِ كابوس، على إنّها مشبّعةٌ بمزيجٍ فريدٍ يجمعُ بين التاريخِ والأساطيرِ والشفافيةِ والغنائيةِ والسخريةِ والسرياليةِ معاً.

استغرقتْ كتابتها اثنتي عشرة سنةً (1984 – 1996)، وكان قد أُجبِرَ خلالَ السنواتِ الثمان من الحربِ العراقيةِ-الإيرانيةِ ليُساقَ جندياً فيها. قُتِلَ أثناءَها العديدُ من أصدقائه. وقد أمضى عدنان ثمانيةَ عشرَ شهراً في موقعِ حجزٍ للجيش، كان عبارةً عن اسطبلٍ مهجورٍ خُزِّنتْ فيه صناديقُ العتاد، قريباً على نحوٍ خطيرٍ من الحدودِ الإيرانية.

في عام 1989، أُعِدّتْ أجزاءٌ من نشيدِ أوروك لتُقدمَ على مسرحِ أكاديميةِ الفنونِ الجميلة. ثمَّ في عام 1993 على مسرحِ الرشيد في بغداد، حيثُ لاقتِ المسرحيةُ استحساناً واسعاً، إلّا إنّها أغضبتِ السلطةَ آنذاك.

فرَّ عدنان وعائلته من البلادِ بحثاً عن ملاذٍ، ابتداءً إلى عمّانَ، ليعقبها الرحيلُ إلى بيروت، ومن ثمَّ السويد، وفي هذهِ المرحلةِ شكّلتْ مقتطفاتٌ من نشيدِ أوروك إلى جانبِ قصائد لصديقهِ الشاعرِ السويدي توماس ترانسترومر (الحائز على جائزة نوبل للآداب)، لتُقدَّمَ منهما أعمالاً مسرحيةً مشتركةً تمَّ عرضها في الأعوام 2006، 2007، 2008، 2014. وكذلك عُرضتْ في مصر عامي 2007، 2008 على التوالي. كما عُرضتْ في المغرب أيضاً في الأعوام 2006، 2007، 2008، 2014.

8

Preface

Uruk's Anthem is one of the longest poems ever written in Arabic
literature (550 pages) and gives voice to the profound despair of the Iraqi
experience. It has been described as beautiful, powerful and courageous –
and at the same time apocalyptic and terrifying in its unwavering scrutiny
of, and opposition to, oppression and dictatorship wherever it occurs in
the world. Fusing ancient Arabic and Sumerian poetic traditions with
many innovative and experimental features of both Arabic and Western
literature, *Uruk's Anthem* might best be described as a modernist dream-
poem that frequently strays into nightmare, yet is also imbued with a
unique blend of history, mythology, tenderness, lyricism, humour and
surrealism. It took twelve years to write (1984–1996). During eight years
of that time Adnan was forced to fight in the Iran–Iraq War. Many of his
friends were killed and he spent eighteen months in an army detention
centre, a disused stable and dynamite store, dangerously close to the
border with Iran.

Parts of *Uruk's Anthem* were adapted for the stage and
performed in 1989 at the Academy of Fine Arts and in 1993 at the
Rasheed Theatre in Baghdad where the play received wide acclaim but
angered the government. Adnan fled the country with his family and
sought asylum first in Amman, then Beirut and then Sweden, where
extracts of *Uruk's Anthem*, together with the poems of Adnan's friend,
the Nobel Laureate Tomas Tranströmer, formed a play which was
performed in 2006, 2007, 2008 and 2014 as well as in Egypt 2007 and
2008. It was also performed in Morocco 2006, 2007, 2008 and 2014.

9

نُشرتْ مقتطفاتٌ من نشيد أوروك لأول مرة باللغة الإنكليزية (ترجمة: جني لويس وربى أبوغيدا) تحت عنوان "غناءٌ لـ إينانا" عن (دار نشر مولفان 2014) كخطوةٍ أولى نحو ترجمةٍ أشمل لهذا النصِّ المهمِ والخالد. ثمَّ أعقبها نشر مقتطفات أخرى في مجلة "القصيدة الطويلة" عام 2016 – العدد 15، وكذلك في مجلة ' King's Review–(كامبرج–2017). ثمَّ نُشرتْ في كتيبٍ مرفقٍ بصور فوتوغرافية للفنان توم هاتون، خريج الكلية الملكية للفنون RCA والحائز على عدة جوائز. كما عُرضتْ أيضاً في معرضٍ رائد بجامعة "كولد سميث" في لندن تحت عنوان "تأثير بلاد ما بين النهرين: النص والتشكيل". وقد ضمَّ المعرض أعمالاً من فنانة الليثوكراف فرانسيس كيرنان، والمصوِّر الفوتوغرافي توم هاتون.

كما قُرئتْ مقاطع من النشيد أيضاً على نطاقٍ واسعٍ في المملكة المتحدة، وفي مهرجاناتِ الشعر الدولية،

كما وشكَّلتْ جزءاً من مسرحية تحتَ عنوان "مَنْ يستطيعُ تَسلُّقَ السماء؟" برعايةِ مجلس الفنون، مع نصوص لجني لويس قامت بإخراجه الفنانة ياسمين سيدوا، صمَّم رقصاته إيتون دالي، حيث قدمت في مهرجان إنخدوانا Enheduanna الذي أُقيم في مالمو – السويد عام 2016، وفي متحف إشموليان Ashmolean في أُكسفورد عام 2017.

وسيتمُّ عرضُ مقتطفاتٍ من نشيد أوروك الى جانب مقتطفاتٍ من قصائد امرئ القيس في مسرحية للمخرج بيتر ستورم، ستقوم بأدائها فرقة Splitmoon المسرحية، وهي قيد الاستعداد لتقديمها في لندن بحلول عام 2021.

أوروك؛ هي مدينة گلگامش، وموقع معبد الإلهة "إينانا". تلك المدينة السومرية التي احتفظتْ باسمها طوال العصر العربي الإسلامي بهيئة "الوركاء".
وقد وُرد ذكرُها في التوراة بصيغة "أوروك"، كما عُرِفتْ عند الإغريق والرومان باسم "أوركي".

ولا تزال بقايا آثارها شاخصةً حتى اليوم شرق العراق، على بعد حوالي 350 كيلومتر جنوب بغداد، على نهر الفرات.

Extracts from *Uruk's Anthem* (translated by Jenny Lewis and Ruba Abughaida) were published in English for the first time in *Singing for Inanna* (Mulfran Press, 2014), a first step towards a fuller translation of this important and historic text. Further extracts were first published in *Long Poem Magazine*, Issue15 (Spring 2016) and in *The King's Review* (Cambridge, 2017), with photographs by award-winning RCA graduate Tom Hatton. These extracts were also featured in a major exhibition, 'Touching Mesopotamia: Text and Texture', at Goldsmiths, University of London, 2018, featuring works by printmaker Frances Kiernan and photographer Tom Hatton. They have also been widely performed in the UK and at international poetry festivals and formed part of an Arts Council-funded theatre piece – *Who Can Climb the Sky?* – directed by Yasmin Sidhwa and choreographed by Euton Daley, performed at the Enheduanna Festival, 2016, Malmo, Sweden and the Ashmolean Museum, Oxford, 2017.

Extracts from *Uruk's Anthem* will also feature with extracts from poems by Imru Al-Qais in a play by Peter Stürm of Splitmoon Theatre Company, currently being developed for performance in London in 2021.

Uruk is the city of Gilgamesh and the site of the temple of the goddess Inanna. It is a Sumerian city that preserved its name all through the Arab Islamic era known as 'Warka'. It is mentioned in the Torah as 'Uruk' and in Greek and Roman as 'Urki'. Its remains today can be found in eastern Iraq, around 350 kilometres south of Baghdad on the Euphrates.

شكر وتقدير

نودُّ أنْ نشكرَ مجلسَ الفنون في إنكلترا على دعمِهِ الوافرِ لترجمةِ مقتطفاتٍ من العمل، من قبل جني لويس وروبي أبو غيدا والتي صدرتُ قبلُ تحت عنوان "غناءٌ لـ اينانا" (عن دار موليفران ، 2014)، ومجلة "القصيدة الطويلة" (العدد 15 ربيع 2016)، ومجلة The King's Review (جامعة كامبريدج 2017).

ونحن أيضاً ممتنون للغايةِ للمترجمين الذين أسهموا إلى حدٍّ كبيرٍ في إبداعِ هذا الكتابِ، وهم:

أماني العبدلي، علي سالم، حسن حجازي، إنعام الشريفي، علاء جمعة، صفاء شيخ حمد، إلين بالستن، د. الياس خميس.

كما نتوجَّهُ بخالصِ شكرنا إلى ليونا ميدلين من دار نشر موليفران التي قامتْ كصديقةٍ ومستشارةٍ بارزةٍ، بدعمِ عملِنا ونشرِهِ في عدَّةِ إصداراتٍ.

بالإضافةِ إلى ذلك نقدمُ الشكرَ للعديد من أصدقائنا الذين تعاونوا معنا: كورينا لوتز، روبي غريفيث، ستيفن واتس، وشعراء الهليار، فيونا بنسون، جون كلارك، جوليا كوبوز، وكلير كروثر، جين درايكوت، آني فرويد، والذين كان لرؤيتِهم لبروفاتِ الترجمةِ أثرٌ نفيسٌ.

وأخيراً، نودُّ أن نشكرَ ماجدة الصائغ ودانة الزبيدي لدعمهما الدائم ولطفهما.

Acknowledgements

We would like to thank Arts Council England for generous grants towards translations of extracts by Jenny Lewis and Ruba Abughaida which have previously appeared in *Singing for Inanna* (Mulfran Press, 2014), *Long Poem Magazine*, Issue 15 (Spring 2016) and *The King's Review*, Cambridge University (2017). We are most grateful also to the following translators who have contributed greatly to the development of this book: Amani Alabdily, Ali Salim, Hassan Hegazy, Inam Alsharifi, Alaa Jima, Safaa Sheikh Hamad, Elin Ballsten and Dr. Elias Khamis. Our sincere thanks go to Leona Medlin, of Mulfran Press, who, as a valued friend and advisor, has championed our work and published it in several editions. Thanks also to our many friends and collaborators including Corinna Lotz and Robbie Griffiths; Stephen Watts, and the Helyars Poets, Fiona Benson, John Clarke, Julia Copus, Claire Crowther, Jane Draycott and Annie Freud whose insights on translated versions have proved invaluable. Finally, we would like to thank Majida Al-Sayegh and Dana Al-Zubaidi for their constant support and kindness.

مقدَّمة
نشيد أوروك، شهادة شاعر

على الرغمِ من الشهرةِ الواسعةِ التي حقَّقَتها القصيدةُ العظيمةُ "نشيدُ أوروك" للشاعر عدنان الصائغ، وصيتها الذائع على مستوى الوطن العربي[1]، إلّا أنّها لم تحظَ بما يستحقُ من تعريفٍ في العالم الغربي – فيما لو استثنينا هذا الكتاب المطبوع من قبل دارِ سيرين للنشرِ، والذي يمثلُ الخُمس من مُجمَل النصِّ الأصليِّ والمُكوَّنِ من 550 صفحة، مما قد يساهمُ بتسليطِ بعضِ الضوءِ.

يُعتبَر الصائغُ، ومنذُ فترةٍ طويلةٍ، أحدَ أبرزِ الشعراءِ الموهوبين من جيلهِ المعروفِ باسمِ "شعراء الثمانينات". يعتمدُ شعرُهُ بشكلٍ عميقٍ على التراثِ القديم للعراق، مستخدماً أساليبَ متنوعةً في الخطابِ. إذ يكمنُ إبداعُهُ في ابتكارِ مزيجٍ متفرِّدٍ من التقنياتِ امتدَّ بين الأنماطِ العربيةِ التقليديةِ والأساليبِ السينمائيةِ والسمعيةِ والحسِّيةِ، بما في ذلك الأصواتِ المتعدِّدة (وغالباً ما تكون متنافرةً)، وكذلك تأرجحه بين التصويرِ العنيفِ تارةً والسورياليِّ تارةً أخرى، من أجلِ خلقِ لغةٍ جديدةٍ، تُنَدِّد وترفضُ الاضطهادَ والقمعَ أينما يحدثُ[2].

أستغرقَ الصائغُ في كتابةِ نشيد أوروك اثني عشر عاماً (1984–1996) – كان قد كَتبَ البعضَ منه أثناءِ فترةِ الخدمةِ الإلزاميةِ في الحربِ العراقيةِ-الإيرانية (1980–1988)، ومنها حينَ وُضِعَ في اسطبلٍ تابعٍ للجيش، والبعضَ الآخرَ حين سكنَ المنفى لاحقاً – ويُنظرُ إليه اليومَ على إنَّهُ إنجازٌ عظيمٌ للصائغ.

إنَّ جزئيةَ القصيدةِ الملحميةِ، وجزئيةَ عواء ألن غينسبرغ من الألمِ والغضبِ، كلاهما يشكِّلان دفقاً مسترسلاً، فريداً، من الوعي المستمدِ من خزينٍ يبدو عندَهُ وكأنْ لا نهايةَ له. نابع من مصادرَ تاريخيةٍ وأُسطوريةٍ وأدبيةٍ، يعزِّزُها تعدُّدُ الثقافاتِ، بدءاً من أساطير بلاد ما بين الرافدين وقصائد ما قبل الإسلام، أو ما تُسمى بالقصائد المعلَّقة[3] (والتي من بينها، أشعار أمرؤ القيس وطرفة بن العبد)،

14

Introduction

Uruk's Anthem, A Poet's Testimony

Despite its wide-reaching fame and notoriety in the Arab world,[1] the
Iraqi poet Adnan Al-Sayegh's monumental poem *Uruk's Anthem* is little
known in the West – an omission that this book from Seren,
representing around twenty per cent of the 550-page original text, will
go some way towards rectifying. Al-Sayegh has long been recognised as
one of the most outstandingly gifted poets of his generation, known in
Iraq as the 'Eighties Poets'. Drawing deeply on the ancient heritage of
Iraq, his poetry uses diverse styles of discourse. Its innovation lies in an
idiosyncratic combination of techniques which range from traditional
Arab forms to filmic, aural and sensory modes, including multiple (often
cacophonous) voices, violent imagery and Surrealism to create a new
language with which to speak out against persecution and oppression
wherever it occurs.[2]

Taking 12 years to write (1984–1996), some of it while he was a
conscripted soldier in the 1980–1988 Iran–Iraq War, some in an Iraqi
military detention centre (a stable) and some later, when he was in exile,
Uruk's Anthem is seen as Al-Sayegh's *magnum opus* to date. Part epic
poem and part Ginsburgian howl of pain and rage, it forms a unique
stream of consciousness drawn from a seemingly bottomless reservoir of
historical, mythical, literary and multi-cultural sources ranging from
Mesopotamian myths, the pre-Islamic Mu'allaqat[3] or 'Hanging Poems,'
(including poets such as Imru Al-Quais and Tarafa ibn Al-'Abd),

ومروراً بالشعراء الصوفيين، أمثال: حافظ والرومي، وصولاً الى المفكرين، والشعراء الحديثين، أمثال: بدر شاكر السياب، محمد الماغوط، عبد الوهاب البياتي، سعدي يوسف، حسب الشيخ جعفر، محمود درويش، أدونيس. على أنَّ هذا هو فقط فيما يتعلق بالشرقِ الأوسط.

علاوةً على ذلك، لا يخلو النصُ من أثرٍ متناغمٍ مع نتاج شعراء غربيين، لطالما حظوا بتقديرٍ عالٍ في العالم العربي، من أمثال: ت. س. إليوت، إديث سيتويل، راينر ماريا ريلكه، آرثر رامبو، فيديريكو غارسيا لوركا، إيميلي ديكنسون، سان جون بيرس[4]، وبالأخص، الشاعر والت ويتمان.

يفيضُ النصُ أيضاً بموجاتٍ فكريةٍ، لو تقفَّينا أثرَها، لوجدناها تنبعُ من تقاليد أوربيةٍ تعودُ للقرنِ الرابع والخامس والسادس عشر تِباعاً، تتعلَّقُ بشعراءٍ ملحميين، وشعراء غنائيين (الشعراء المتجولين)، ومنها ما يتعلَّقُ برواياتٍ تتحدَّث عن الصعاليك للروائي ثيربانتس. إنَّ عنصرَ الحلمِ ورؤية الحلمِ في نشيد أوروك هي أداةٌ أدبيةٌ تعودُ إلى أبعد من ذلكَ – من خلالِ كوميديا الأخطاء لـ دانتي، وعزاء الفلسفة لـ بوثيوس، والأحلام والنُذُر لـ فرجيل في قصيدته "الإنيَاذة". وفي نهايةِ المطافِ خِبَاء الرؤى التي صنعها أنكيدو في المكانِ ذاتِهِ الذي تلقَّى فيه گلگامش الإشاراتِ والنذورَ القادمةَ من القمرِ بواسطةِ إلهِ الأحلامِ "زاكار"، في أولِ قطعةٍ أدبيةٍ مدوَّنةٍ في العالمِ، متمثلةٍ بـ "ملحمة گلگامش". فبمجرَّدِ أن يغلقَ راوي نشيد أوروك عينيه مستغرقاً في نومٍ عميقٍ، حتى تستحيلَ أحلامُهُ إلى هلوساتٍ.

رأيتُ الكواكبَ تسجدُ لي

والقيامةَ ذاتِ البروقِ تضجُّ بحشدِ العَرايا

تفوجُ بسيلِ الخطايا...

واسرافيلَ ينفخُ في بوقِهِ:

انهضوا يا نيامَ القرونِ الكسيحةِ...

صحتُ: أينَ الإلهُ؟ (ص.62).

16

Sufi poets such as Hafez and Rumi, through to modern thinkers and poets such as Badr Shakir Al-Sayyab, Muhammad Al-Maghut, Abd Wahab Al-Bayati, Saadi Youssef, Hasab Al-Sheikh Jafar, Mahmoud Darwish and Adonis; and this is only the Middle Eastern contingent.

Additionally, many Western resonances weave through the text with poets who are admired in the Arab world such as T.S. Eliot, Edith Sitwell, Rainer Maria Rilke, Arthur Rimbaud, Federico García Lorca, Emily Dickinson, Saint-John Perse[4] and, especially, Walt Whitman. There are also streams of thought that can be traced back to 14th, 15th and 16th century European traditions of bards, troubadours and the picaresque novels of Cervantes. The element of dream and dream vision in *Uruk's Anthem* is a literary device that goes back even further – through Dante's *The Divine Comedy*, Boethius' *The Consolation of Philosophy,* the dreams and portents of Virgil's *Aeneid* and, ultimately, the dream tents made by Enkidu in which Gilgamesh receives signs and omens, brought from the moon by Zaqar, god of dreams, in the first piece of written literature in the world, the *Epic of Gilgamesh*. In *Uruk's Anthem*, after closing his eyes and falling deeply asleep, the narrator's dreams are hallucinatory –

> I saw the planets kneeling to me
> and the resurrection, ablaze with lightning, crammed with naked
> crowds overflowing with their mistakes...
> and Israfil blew his horn:
> *Wake up you sleeping people from your crippled centuries!*
> I shouted: *Where is God?* (p.63).

غالباً ما تتلاقى رؤى الحلم بتجسيدٍ للفضائلِ والرذائلِ، أو للمفاهيمِ المجرّدةِ، كاليأسِ أو الحزنِ أو الموتِ. لذا من الممكنِ النظرُ إلى فريقِ العملِ الضخمِ في مسرحِ عدنان الفسيح – والمكوّنِ من الآلهةِ، الآلهاتِ، الملوكِ، المحظيّاتِ، الأبطالِ، الأشرارِ، الجنودِ، الجنرالاتِ، الأطباءِ الجرّاحين، حرّاسِ السجون، أدلاءِ المتاحفِ، العاهراتِ، نُدُلِ الحاناتِ، الشعراءِ، الفلاسفةِ، الفتياتِ العابثاتِ، النساءِ الغامضاتِ، وبشكلٍ عرضيٍّ الفئرانِ والقططِ والحيتان – على أنّهُ فريقُ عملٍ مجازيٍّ، يصوّرُ مقطعاً عرضياً للحياةِ، يمكنُ التعرّفُ عليه ضمن أيةِ فترةٍ من التاريخِ أو عبرَ أيةِ ثقافةٍ.

كما يهيمنُ على إطارِ النصِّ برمّتِهِ إحساسُ "الحالمِ"؛ إنّهُ ذلكَ الشاعرُ الحائرُ والذاهلُ[5]، كمَن أُقحِمَ أعزلاً في عالمٍ بائسٍ.

فقد وجدَ نفسَهُ أولَ الأمرِ، عالقاً وسطَ مجتمعٍ يعاني من انهيارٍ كارثيٍّ بسببِ العنفِ الذي ألحقهُ به النظامُ الاستبداديُّ، ليعقبَهُ رعبُ الحربِ الذي لا يُوصفُ.

هذا هو العالمُ الذي بُتِرتْ فيه روحُ الشاعرِ الشابِ من جذورِها الطبيعيةِ قبلَ أن تُمسي غربةُ المنفى وابتعادُهُ عن بلادِهِ واقعاً دائماً.

في دراسةِ البروفسور هناء خلِّيف غني[6]، التي تناولتْ تجربةَ الصائغ باعتبارِه شاعراً منفياً، اقتبست عن يوربيديس (روائي مسرحي يوناني) في مسرحية "النساء الفينيقيات" – جوكاستا: ما معنى أن يُنفى المرءُ من بلادِه؟، هل هو بلاءٌ عظيمٌ؟ يجيبُها بولينيسيس: إنَّ الأعظمُ، والأصعبُ، في تحملِهِ أكثر من البوح به".

إنّهُ تذكيرٌ في الوقتِ المناسبِ، في ظلِّ عصرِ النزوحِ العالميِّ هذا، بأنَّ أولئكَ الذين لمْ يختبروا المنفى، لنْ يكونَ لديهم سوى القليلِ من الفهمِ الحقيقيِّ للمشاعرِ المتضاربةِ التي تنشأ بين أولئكَ الذين خبروهُ.

إنَّ صدمةَ الحربِ، والسأمَ، ولاجدوى المنفى (مهما كان امتنانُ المُغترِب ربما للضيافةِ المَديدةِ التي يقدّمُها له البلدُ الجديدُ) ستغدو مشاعرَ تستوطنهُ، حتى لتستحيلَ الى حالةٍ ضمنيةٍ دائمةٍ للوعي.

الصائغُ نفسُهُ يقولُ في قصيدتِهِ: "خرجتُ من الحربِ سهواً"، ليدخلَ في

Just as in dream visions encounters are often with personifications of virtues, vices or abstract concepts such as despair or grief, so the teeming cast of Al-Sayegh's vast theatre – the gods, goddesses, kings, concubines, heroes, villains, soldiers, generals, surgeons, prison guards, museum attendants, prostitutes, barmen, poets, philosophers, flirting girls, mysterious women and occasional rats, cats and whales could be seen as allegorical, representing a cross section of life that we can recognise from any period of history and from any culture. Dominating the atmosphere throughout is the sense of the 'dreamer', the 'bewildered and unaware poet',[5] thrust defenceless into a dystopian world, first of a society undergoing catastrophic breakdown from the violence inflicted on it by a tyrannical regime, then the unspeakable horror of war. This is a world in which the spirit of the young poet was severed from its natural roots long before the estrangement of physical exile from his own country became a lasting reality.

In his paper on Al-Sayegh's experiences as an exiled poet, Professor Hana Khliaf Ghena[6] quotes from Euripides' *The Phoenician Women* – 'Jocasta: *What means exile from one's country? Is it a great evil?* / Polyneices: *The greatest; harder to bear than tell.*' A timely reminder, in this age of global displacement, that those of us who have not experienced exile can have little true understanding of the conflicting feelings it engenders among those who have. The trauma of war and the boredom and pointlessness of exile (however grateful the refugee may be for the hospitality extended by their new country) becomes a permanently internalised state of consciousness. Al-Sayegh himself says, in his poem 'I Emerged from the War Unawares', that he enters the

"... مدارِ القصيدةِ، نصفَ طليقٍ، ونصفَ مصفَّد"[7]، أي أنَّ نصفَهُ حُرٌّ، له أن يَكتبَ ويستمتعَ بحياتِهِ. غير أنَّ ثمةَ نصفاً آخرَ لا يزالُ مقيَّداً بهشيمِ الروحِ المحطَّمةِ بسببِ الماضي. ليس له القدرةُ لأنْ يعودَ إلى ذلكَ الشخصِ الذي كان عليهِ يوماً، ولا إلى وطنِهِ الذي أحبَّهُ.

حتى وإنْ حاولَ إيصالَ هذه الحقيقةِ النافرةِ إلى تخومِ العالمِ من خلالِ شِعرِهِ.

ثمَّةَ تشابهٌ واضحٌ بين شعرِ الصائغ وأعمالِ معارضين آخرين – على سبيلِ الذكرِ الشاعر الفلسطيني محمود درويش، والشاعر اليوناني يانيس ريتسوس. فعندما سُئلَ الصائغُ في المؤتمرِ الذي أُستضيف فيه في آسفي بالمغرب عام 2015، والذي دامَ أربعةَ أيامٍ، حولَ شعرِ المقاومةِ: "هل إنَّ الشعرَ هو فعلٌ ثوري؟". أظهرتِ الآراءُ وقتئذٍ شيئاً من التوافقِ المُفضي الى أنَّ شِعرَ المعارضةِ قد قطعَ شوطاً طويلاً بعيداً عن جذورِهِ الأصليةِ التي نبعثْ من الماركسيةِ، كما ترجمها شعراء من أمثالِ نيرودا ولوركا الذين كانوا يكتبون ضدَّ الإمبريالية والاستعمار. على أنَّ هدفَهُ الأساسيَّ لا يزالُ هو ذاتَهُ – التعبير عن المعارضةِ، والتعريفِ بشجاعةِ الفردِ في النضالِ من أجلِ حريةِ القولِ والفكرِ. وكما جاءَ بقولِ ريتسوس: "بعيداً عن الحريةِ لنْ يتحقَّقَ شيءٌ"[8].

كانتْ هناك عدَّةُ بحوثٍ تسعى إلى مقارنةِ شعرِ الصائغ بشعراء الحرب ممنْ ينتمون إلى لائحةِ الأثرِ الغربي. وقد كان ويلفريد أوين[9] خياراً واضحاً. إذ شرعَ كلاهما بكتابةِ الشعرِ في بواكيرِ شبابِهما. كما أنَّ كليهما عانى أقصى درجاتِ الرعبِ في الحربِ، رافقَ ذلك إحساسٌ بالخذلانِ الروحيِّ. على أنَّ أوين صبَّ جُلَّ غضبِهِ على الإنسانيةِ (أوِ انعدامِها)، وعلى الإلهِ. ففي قصيدةِ "الحب الأعظم"، والتي كتبها الشاعرُ على الأرجحِ بين نوفمبر 1917 – يناير 1918 في كريفكورت، والتي كانتْ ردًّا على قصيدةِ الشاعر ألغيرنون تشارلز سوينبورن "قبلَ المرآة"، سعى أوينُ من خلالِها الى إحياءِ إحساسِنا بالموتِ

20

'…orbit of the poem / Half free / And half in shackles',[7] that is, half free to write and enjoy his new life, yet half still handcuffed to the spiritual devastation of the past and his inability to return to the person he once was and the homeland he loves. Through his poetry he attempts to communicate this alienated reality to the rest of the world.

There are obvious similarities between Al-Sayegh's poetry and the work of other dissidents such as the Palestinian poet Mahmoud Darwish and the Greek poet Yannis Ritsos. At a four day conference on the poetry of resistance in Safi, Morocco in 2015, at which Al-Sayegh was a guest speaker, the question was asked: 'Is poetry a revolutionary act?' What emerged was a consensus that the poetry of resistance has moved on a long way from its original roots in Marxism as interpreted by poets such as Neruda and Lorca who were writing against imperialism and colonialism; yet its fundamental purpose is still the same – to voice dissent and testify to the courage of the individual in fighting for freedom of speech and thought. As Ritsos says 'Without freedom there is nothing'.[8]

There have been several attempts to compare Al-Sayegh's poetry to war poets from the Western canon, Wilfred Owen[9] being an obvious choice. Both were young men when they started writing. Both suffered the extremities of horror in war, with its attendant sense of spiritual abandonment. Owen's outrage is against both humanity (or lack of it) and God. In 'Greater Love', probably drafted between November 1917–January 1918 at Craiglockhart, in response to Swinburne's poem 'Before the Mirror', Owen reconstructs the scene for us of the dead and

والفناءِ: "طرفُ السكّينِ الأعمى، أنّها تواصلُ تدحرجَها، وعلى ما يبدو، أنَّ اللهَ غيرُ مكترثٍ..." (ص.143) [10]. لما كانَ نداءُ الوطنِ "وديعاً، والمساءَ صافياً"، باتَ الجنودُ صامتين في ساحاتِ القتالِ – "فقد آنَ للأرضِ أنْ تَمنعَ أفواهَهم البائسةَ من السعالِ". نستشعرُ غضبَ الشاعرِ هنا بقوةٍ محسوسةٍ، كما اعتادَ أنْ يفعلَ كلّما اعتزمَ الحديثَ عن الموتى.

وبالطريقةِ نفسِها، يترجمُ "نشيد أوروك" صوتَ الشاعرِ معتزماً البوحَ دونَ خوفٍ، وبأيِّ ثمنٍ، ضدَ القهرِ والقسوةِ والاضطهاد –

حتى وإنْ أحسَّ بتهميشِ صوتِه.

صحتُ: اتركوني أقصُّ لكم ما رأيتُ...

فلم يمنحوني انتباهاً

وراحَ الخبيرُ يُفصّلُني – فوقَ مَشْرحَةِ النّصِّ

(ص.62).

وكما هو الحالُ مع أوينَ الذي ينبّهنا في قصيدتِه "الحالات العقلية" بأنَّ استحالةَ محوِ الذكرياتِ تؤدي إلى ما نسمّيه اليومَ بـ "اضطراب ما بعدَ الصدمة" (PTSD). وهو ما عُرفَ خلالَ فترةِ الحربِ 1914–1918 باسمِ "صدمة القصف". هنا أيضاً، يهتمُ الصائغُ بعواقبِ الحربِ والإرهابِ تماماً كاهتمامِه بالعواقبِ الفعليةِ. ولعلّ العديدَ من أولئك الذين عانوا من هذا الاضطرابِ النفسيِّ، لمْ يتمكنوا من ممارسةِ حياتِهم الطبيعةِ مرةً أخرى .

"أنّهم يرون ذاتَ الأشياءِ دوماً، ويسمعونَ أصواتِها، دوي القنابلِ، وتشظّي العضلاتِ المتطايرةِ، إنّها مجزرةٌ لا تُضاهى..." (ص.146).

في قصيدةِ "المُعاق" والتي تتحدّثُ عن جسدٍ محطّمٍ برمّتِه لفتى محاربٍ يجلسُ

"... على كرسيٍّ متحرّكٍ، يترقّبُ الظلامَ،

... دونَ ساقين، مُخيّطاً بضعفٍ إلى المرفقِ".

dying with 'limbs knife-skewed, / Rolling and rolling there / Where God seems not to care…'(p.143).[10] Whereas the voices of home are 'Gentle, and evening clear', the soldiers on the battlefield have been silenced – 'Now earth has stopped their piteous mouths that coughed.' The anger of the poet reaches us with palpable force as does his determination to speak for the dead. In the same way, *Uruk's Anthem* shows the voice of the poet resolved to speak out, at all costs, against injustice, cruelty and oppression – even when he feels his voice is ignored –

> I shouted: *Let me tell you what I saw!*
> but they wouldn't listen
> and the professor began cutting me – over a morgue of text
> (p.63).

Like Owen, Al-Sayegh is as concerned with the aftermath of war and terror as with the actual events. In 'Mental Cases' Owen reminds us of how the impossibility of erasing memories results in what we would today call Post Traumatic Stress Disorder (PTSD). During the 1914–18 War it was known as shellshock, and many of those who suffered from it would never again know a state of normality – 'Always they must see these things and hear them, / Batter of guns and shatter of flying muscles, / Carnage incomparable…' (p.146). In 'Disabled' it is the body that is irrevocably shattered. The young war veteran sits '…in a wheeled chair, waiting for dark /…Legless, sewn short at the elbow.'

إذ يتعاطفُ أوينُ هنا مع العائدين من اللاحياة.

الليلةَ لاحظَ كيفَ أنَّ عيونَ النساء
تنتقلُ منه إلى الرجالِ الأقوياءِ الذين كانوا متكاملين.
كَمْ كانَ ذلكَ قاسياً! لماذا لا يأتون
ويضعونهُ في السريرِ؟ لماذا لا يأتون؟ (ص.152–153).

أمَّا من وجهةِ نظرِ الصائغِ، فإنَّهُ يرى فيما لو كانَ الخَيارُ للمرءِ أنْ يَقتُلَ أو أنْ يُقتَلَ. حينها
يغدو "كلٌّ يحملُ موتَ الآخرِ" في راحتيهِ، وليسَ ذلك فحسبُ، بلْ يحملُ أيضاً مصيرَ
عائلةِ الضحيةِ في القادمِ من الأيامِ. ربما ثمَّة فتاةٌ صغيرةٌ بانتظارِ والدِها، أو صبيٌّ يترقَّبُ
عودةَ والدِهِ إلى البيت.

[كان القنَّاصُ] المتأرجحُ في حبلٍ مشدودٍ بين الموتِ وعنقِ المهزولِ.
رأيتُ شرائطَها، مرجَ طفولاتٍ وزنابقَ تخفقُ في
الريحِ أمامي، وتطولُ، تطولُ – متى يأتي
بابا؟ يقطعُها صوتُ قطارٍ ينحبُ... هل يأتي بابا؟
لا أدري، لا أدري، كلٌّ يحملُ موتَ الآخرِ في
كفَّيهِ... أتسمعُني يا هذا القنَّاصُ الأبلهُ: كلٌّ يحملُ بين
أصابعِهِ المشدودةِ فوقَ زنادِ الرشاشةِ، أرملةً ويتيماً... (ص.116، 118).

ثمَّةَ تساؤلٌ يراودُ المرءَ بشأنِ الإيمانِ باللهِ، يتزامنُ مع تلاشي الإيمانِ بتحقيقِ
مجتمعٍ عادلٍ. من وجهةِ نظرِ أوينَ، فإنَّهُ أشارَ إلى ضرورةِ نشرِ الأفكارِ من خلالِ نصوصٍ
حداثويةٍ لما بعد الحربِ العالميةِ الأولى، وكمثالٍ على ذلك قصيدة إليوت "الأرض
اليَباب": "يا ابن آدم، / ... لأنَّك لا تعرفُ غيرَ كومةٍ من مُكسَّرِ الأصنامِ" (من "دفن
الموتى") [ت: د. عبد الواحد لؤلؤة].

24

Owen empathises with the non-life to come –

> Tonight he noticed how the women's eyes
> Passed from him to the strong men who were whole.
> How cold it is! Why don't they come
> And put him to bed? Why don't they come? (pp.152–153).

For Al-Sayegh, it is the knowledge that, with the option of kill or be killed, not only is each soldier 'carrying the death of the other' in his palms but also the future fate of the victim's family – the little girl waiting for her daddy, or the son waiting for his dad, to come home.

> [The sniper] was swinging on the rope between death and my weak neck. I saw her ribbon like a meadow of childhood and lilies fluttering in the wind in front of me, it got longer and longer – *when will my Daddy come?* interrupted by the wailing of a train... *when will Dad come?*
> I don't know, I don't know, each is carrying the death of the other in his palms...do you hear me you doltish sniper: each carries between his gripping fingers and the gun trigger, a widow and an orphan. (pp.117, 119).

With the waning of faith in a just society there also comes a questioning of faith in God, a perspective which, in Owen's case, presages themes in post-First World War modernist texts like Eliot's 'The Waste Land': 'Son of man, / ...you know only/ A heap of broken images,' (*The Burial of the Dead*).

مع ادراكِ الصائغ بفاعليةِ قصيدةِ "الأرض اليباب" على شعرِه. إلّا أنّهُ سيكونُ من الخطأِ رسمُ أيةِ مقارنةٍ قريبةٍ بين كاتبٍ أو حركةٍ غربيين مع مُنجز الصائغ الشعريّ هذا.

ورُبّما كان أقربُ نظيرٍ لشعرِ الصائغ يمكنُ استنباطهُ من الثقافةِ الغربيةِ هي عملُ الشاعرِ الآنجلو- ويلزي ديفيد جونز "بين قوسين" (نص عرفهُ الصائغ مؤخراً فقط). وقد سبقَ أن كلُّ به كلٌّ من الشاعرين ت. س. إليوت و وليام بتلر ييتس، باعتباره منجزاً عبقرياً.

وهذا العملُ يشتركُ في العديدِ من سماتِه مع نشيد أوروك.

يتشكّلُ نشيدُ أوروك بشكلٍ كبيرٍ على أساطيرِ الشرقِ الأوسطِ والحكاياتِ الشعبيةِ بما فيها ألف ليلةٍ وليلةٍ، ملحمة گلگامش، قصة الخلقِ البابلية "إينوما إيليش"، ملحمة "أترا هاسس". في ذاتِ الوقتِ يصفُ ديفيد جونز قصيدتَهُ "بين قوسين" بأنّها "مزيجٌ" من تراثِه المتماوجِ[11] بين الثقافةِ الويلزيةِ والإنجليزية. والتي كان أن تقدّمَ لها من خلالِ بضعِ صفحاتٍ صورةً عن حكايا ويلز القديمةِ والمعروفةِ بـ "مابينوغون" (من أقدمِ قصصِ النثرِ البريطاني) وكذلك أشعار "تالييسن"، رواية الخيال والفروسية لـ "مالوري آرثر"، التقاليد الرومانسية السائدة في العصورِ الوسطى، بريطانيا الرومانية، كتابَي العهد القديم والجديد، شكسبير، لائحة الشعراء الغربيين برمّتهم، والأهم من ذلك كلّه، هو لغةُ الرُقباءِ والعُرفاء. وبالدرجةِ الأولى جنود كوكني الذين حاربوا إلى جانبِه حتى أُصيبَ في يونيو 1917 في معركةِ "سوم" (بلدة فرنسية). في الوقتِ الذي فيه روايةُ جونز حالةَ ارتقاءِ الأنا البديلةِ المتمثّلةِ بشخصيةِ الجندي جون بول، نجدُنا نقتفي أثرَ عبود في نشيد أوروك بشكلٍ متقطّعٍ.

– وعَبُّودُ أين؟
عَبُّودُ في السجنِ يركُلُهُ الحارسُ الفظُّ (ص.118).

بينما يوشكُ أنْ يكونَ النصُّ "بين قوسين" أقربَ للنثرِ، يُوظِّفُ نشيدُ أوروك مختلفَ الأشكالِ الشعريةِ، منتهجاً في سياقِهِ أسلوبَ البلاغةِ، بالإضافةِ الى التكرارِ (الجِناس[12] على وجهِ الخصوصِ)، إضافةً الى النثرِ. لقد عمدَ كلاهما إلى استخدامِ

26

Al-Sayegh acknowledges the influence of 'The Waste Land' on his own poetry; yet it would be wrong to draw too close a comparison to any single Western writer or movement on his work. Perhaps the nearest parallel that can be drawn from Western culture is with the Anglo-Welsh poet David Jones's *In Parenthesis* (a text that Al-Sayegh has only recently become aware of). Hailed by T.S. Eliot and W.B. Yeats, among others, as a work of genius it shares many of the dominating features of *Uruk's Anthem*. Whereas *Uruk's Anthem* draws heavily on Middle Eastern myths and folk tales, including *The 1001 Arabian Nights, The Epic of Gilgamesh, Enuma Elish* and *Atra-Hasis*, David Jones describes *In Parenthesis* as a 'hotchpotch'[11] of his own mixed heritage of Welsh and English cultures which, in a few pages, can draw on the old Welsh tales of *The Mabinogi* and the poems of Taliesin, Malory's *Morte d'Arthur* and the medieval Romance tradition, Roman Briton, the Old and New Testaments, Shakespeare, the whole of the Western canon of poets and, most importantly, the language of the sergeants, corporals and predominantly Cockney soldiers he fought alongside until he was wounded in June 1917 at the Battle of the Somme. Jones's narrative depicts the progress of his alter ego, Private John Ball, whereas in *Uruk's Anthem*, it is Aboud whose story we follow sporadically –

> *– And where is Aboud?*
> Aboud is in prison, getting kicked by the vicious guard. (p.119).

While *In Parenthesis* is mostly in prose, *Uruk's Anthem* employs many different types of poetic and rhetorical forms including repetition (especially anaphora)[12] as well as prose. Both use copious instances of

أسلوبٌ زاخرٌ بالتباينِ اللغويِّ، من خلالِ مزجِ مقاطعَ مختلفةٍ وإثرائِها بنتفٍ من الأغاني وأنصافٍ من الأقوالِ المأثورةِ، لخلقِ لفظٍ جديدٍ أكثرَ تعبيراً.

يخبرُنا جونز أنَّهُ وبسببِ قوانينِ الرقابةِ "كان مقيَّداً بالأعرافِ التي منعتهُ من استخدامِ كلماتٍ غيرِ لائقةٍ، وآثمةٍ في النصِّ". على الرغمِ من حقيقةِ أنَّ لغةَ الجنديِ التي كانَ يستخدمُها لا تخلو من الشتائمِ والفظاظةِ، لكنْ كانَ لابدَّ من تنقيتِها. من ناحيةٍ أخرى، يستخدمُ الصائغُ صوراً مثيرةً فاضحةً وجنسيةً متواترةً[13]. وهذا هو أحدُ الأسبابِ، بالإضافةِ إلى التطرقِ إلى السياسةِ والدينِ، لجعلِ الكتابِ محظوراً أو يتعرضُ للقصِّ في بعضِ الدولِ العربيةِ.

(– هل عِنْدَكِ كبريت؟
– لا) قادتني في عتمةِ دهليزٍ،
أتَلَمَّسُ ردفيها وطريقي المتعثِّرَ...
رغم العتمةِ أبصرتُ فحيحَ الرغبةِ في عينيها السوداوين ونصفَ الزِّرِّ المقطوعِ...
(– البارحةَ انقطعَ التيارُ) دنوتُ من الأزرارِ الأخرى. (ص.112).

غالباً ما تقترنُ الإيروتيكية بمقاطعَ غنائيةٍ :

أزحفُ بين القبورِ وألغامِنا، فأُحِسُّ دبيبَ أغانيكِ خافتةً في صفيرِ الرياحِ
تهدهدُ ليلَ القرى الغافياتِ
(ثيابي مُبلَّلَةٌ بنديفِ الغيومِ. وقلبي ملاذُ العصافيرِ. (ص.158، 160).

أو رثاءِ القلبِ الممزَّقِ –
قلتُ: انتظرتُكَ...
نمضي معاً في الأزِّقَةِ (لا بيتَ لي
غيرُ ظلِّ القصيدةِ

heteroglossia – mixing different registers with snatches of song and half-spoken sentences to form a fluent kind of new utterance. Because of censorship laws, Jones says he was 'hampered by the convention of not using impious and impolite words'.[13] Despite the fact that the soldier's lingo he was using was actually peppered with swearing and crudity, it had to be cleaned up. Al-Sayegh, on the other hand, uses frequent bawdy, scatological and sexual images which is another of the reasons, in addition to touching on politics and religion, that the book is banned or expurgated in some Arab countries:

> (– *Have you got a light?*
> – *No*). She led me into a dark passage,
> I was feeling her buttocks in my stumbling way.
> Despite darkness, I saw lust hissing in her black eyes and half a
> button…(yesterday the electricity was off) I undid the other
> buttons. (p.113).

Eroticism is often juxtaposed with lyrical passages –

> I crawl between the graves and our mines, sensing the tread of
> your soft songs subdued beneath the whistle of a wind that
> lulls the nights of sleeping villages (my clothes wet with clouds
> and my heart a haven for finches… (pp.159, 161).

or heart-rending pathos –

> I said: *I waited for you…*
> *to wander with you in the alleys* (there's no home for me
> except the shade of a poem,

أفرشُهُ وأنامُ)

شريدين،

تُنكِرُنا واجهاتُ الفنادقِ

والطرقاتُ الغريبةُ

متكئاً فوق كَتفي،

يُبلِّلُ دمعُك عُشبَ قميصي

تُحَدِّثُني عن مسارِ الغيومِ بجفنيكَ

عن جوعِ طفليكَ في بلدِ النخلِ...

(ص.166، 168).

ويأتي التحوّلُ الفجائيُّ في نبرةِ النصِّ، ليكونَ له مثل تأثيرِ القَطعِ السينمائيِّ. وبالتالي يزعزعُ مسارَ السردِ، ويلتقطُ الحالةَ الذهنيةَ المشظّاةَ للجنديِّ الذي كانَ، أو السجينَ، أو المنفي لاحقاً.

نجدُ أنَّ جونز يحثُّنا على التمعُّنِ المستفيضِ في قراءةِ الهوامشِ الغزيرةِ في قصيدتِهِ "بين قوسين". وهو ذاتُ الصدى الذي ردَّدَهُ الصائغُ في هذا الديوان. كلاهما يشعرُ بأنَّ معرفةَ تلكَ المؤثراتِ "الكامنة"، أمرٌ أشبهُ بمياهٍ عميقةٍ "مقلقةٍ" تجري تحتَ النصِّ المكتوبِ[14]، وهي ضروريةٌ لتحقيقِ ذروةِ المتعةِ في عملِهما.

إنَّ أولئكَ الذين يستفيضون في قراءةِ هذا النصِّ فإنَّهم سيخرجون بأقصى جدوى من هذهِ المقتطفاتِ لنشيدِ أوروك، فضلاً عن الوصولِ بعيداً في فهمِ مدى الإثراءِ من ذلكَ التلاقحِ المتبادلِ لآلافِ السنين من موروثاتِ الشرقِ الأوسطِ، والغربِ، وهو تماماً ما تُمثِّلُهُ هذه القصيدةُ الآسرةُ والمُلهمةُ.

جني لويس

أكسفورد 2020/4/8

ترجمة: أماني العبدلي

which I throw to the ground like a mat to sleep on);

we are homeless,

hotels reject us

and strange roads

rest on my shoulders,

your tears wet my shirt

your eyelids tell me about the movement of clouds,

about the hunger of your two children in the land of palm trees.

(pp.167, 169).

These sudden shifts in tone, like cinematic jump cuts, have the effect of destabilising the narrative and capturing the fragmented state of mind of the soldier, prisoner or exile.

Jones implores us to take time to read the copious endnotes in *In Parenthesis* – a plea echoed by Al-Sayegh in this book. Both feel that knowledge of the 'subterranean' influences, like deep water 'troubling' beneath the written text,[14] are essential to one's full engagement with their work. Those who take time to comply with this request will not only gain the most from these extracts from *Uruk's Anthem,* but they will also come away from the experience with a far better understanding of the rich cross-fertilisation between thousands of years of Middle Eastern and Western traditions that this compelling and visionary poem represents.

Jenny Lewis

Oxford, 8 April, 2020

نشيد اوروك

[أجلسُ في شُرفةِ الصحو،

أنتفُ ريشَ الغمامِ

شفاهي مشقَّقةٌ كجذوعِ النخيلِ على الجرفِ

أرقبُ خوفو[15]،

وحيداً،

– على قِمَّةِ الهَرمِ المستدقَّةِ –

يكرعُ خمرةَ شعبٍ أُبيدَ...

حزيناً،

يُقلِّبُ طرفيه بين عظامِ الهياكلِ...

يهتفُ: يا شعبُ...

لا شيءَ، غيرُ صدى حجرٍ

يتدحرجُ جُ جُ جُ جُ جُ

جُ جُ جُ

جُ جُ

جُ

... في البئرِ

يزعقُ:

... يا جندُ

يقفزُ – بين شقوقِ الحجارةِ –

جرذٌ سمينٌ

يجرُّ بقايا ذراعِ فتاةٍ... فيفزعُ خوفو...

ويهبطُ

في السُّلَّمِ الحلزونيِّ،

يغلقُ بوَّابةَ القصرِ

ثمَّ يموتُ

Uruk's Anthem

I sit on the balcony, alert;

I pluck the feathers of clouds,

    my lips are cracked like the roots of the palm tree on the bank.

    I see Khofu[15]

        alone

            on top of the pyramid's spire

gulping the dregs of a massacred people…

sad,

sweeping his gaze over the skeletons' bones…

he shouts: *O people…!*

there is nothing but the echo of the rocks

he rolls s s s s s s s s s

           sss

          ss

            s

                 …into the well.

He yells:

…*O soldiers!*

He jumps – between the cracks of the rocks –

a fat rat

drags chunks of a girl's arms…(so Khofu panics

and hurries down

the spiral staircase,

locks the door of the palace

then dies,

وحيداً...] رأيتُ الطرائدَ في شَبَكِ الاتساعِ

رأيتُ دمي في الرقيمِ

إلى جنبِهِ كاتمُ الصوتِ

يلمعُ مبتسماً

ويصافحُني بحياءٍ

رأيتُ جهازَ التنصُّتِ،

ملتصقاً بصدورِ الصبيَّاتِ،

يردحنَ في الحفلاتِ

رأيتُ الحدائقَ مهجورةً

في غيابِكِ

والدودَ أصفرَ يدبي إليَّ

رأيتُ دماءَ العبيدِ

على حجرِ المعبدِ السومريِّ

يطنُّ عليها ذبابُ العصورِ

رأيتُ إلى العصرِ يسقطُ

من ناطحاتِ السحابِ

رأيتُ "الخيامَ"

— بحانةِ شيرازَ —

يحسو كؤوسَ الوجودِ،

وينسى الحساب

رأيتُ الكتابَ

— بأسواقِ اسبارطةَ —

بُحَّ:

مَنْ يشتريني؟

رأيتُ أبي نائماً

— فوق محراثِهِ —

ولصوصَ الحكومةِ ينتهبون سنابلَهُ والأغاني

34

alone...) I saw the prey in a wide net,

I see my blood etched on a clay tablet

and next to it, a silenced revolver

      shakes my hand shyly

         with a gleaming smile.

I saw bugging devices

   slipped into the cleavage of girls

      dancing at parties.

I saw gardens made empty

by your absence

and yellow worms crawling towards me.

I saw the blood of slaves

     on a Sumerian stone altar –

        the flies of ages buzzing round it.

I saw time fall

from the high-rises.

I saw Khayyam

     – In Shiraz's bar –

sipping cups of existence

      and forgetting to keep score.

I saw books piled high

     in the markets of Sparta –

     rasping

       Who will buy me?

I saw my father sleeping

    on his plough

and government thieves looting his stalks and songs.

رأيتُ البروقَ الطروقَ تَشُقُّ بحَربتِها

بطنَ قنطور

حتى تدلَّتْ مع الكَرْمِ أمعاؤُهُ،

وبعوضَ إيزوبوس يَحْمِلُ جثثَنا

ويطيرُ..

زُزُزُزُز

رأيتُ المَعَرّي[16] يقدّمُ أشعارَهُ علفاً للجوامِ

يسِ

في خطئي فكرةٌ أنتَ أخطأتَها في التفقّهِ

حتى استطالتْ حبالاً لشنقي.

تركنا الحقائبَ فارغةً كالحقائق

فوقَ رصيفِ مدائنِ نيبور[17] كي نلحقَ

القاطراتِ

التي

مضغتْ تبنَ تاريخنا،

فتجشَّأ ثغرُ المذيعةِ حين رأتنا نُؤجِّجُ

ثوراتِنا بالكلامِ،

فقامتْ

لتولعَ

سيجارَها الماليبورو...

ووووووووو

فالتهبَ القَشُ تحتَ الأرائكِ،...

ثمَّ أضافتْ:

[وصرّحَ في الاجتماعِ المُدارِ

وزيرُ الحصارِ: (لقد نفدَ الزيتُ – يا سادتي –

في مخازنِ دولتِنا،

فليقلِّ المواطنُ بيضتَهُ

بالضراطِ...)...

36

I saw lightning strike, splitting open with its blade

the belly of the centaur

so its guts dangled in the vineyard,

> and Eusebius' mosquitoes carrying our corpses

> and flying

> zzzzz

I saw Al–Mu'ari[16] feed his poems to the buff –

> a-lo –

Inside my mistake was an idea you twisted

until it stretched into a rope to hang me.

We dumped the bags, empty as truth,

on a hard street by Naybur's[17] ziggurats and followed

> the carts

> that were munching our history as if it was hay

The presenter vomited when she saw us light

our revolution with words

and rose

to light

a Marlboro

> o o o o o o o

the straw caught fire under the sofas

then she added:

[a declaration from the meeting chaired by

> the Minister of Siege: *Gentlemen,*

our stocks of oil have run out

so now citizens have to fry their eggs

> *with farts...*

وقامَ ليشرَحَ

فامتعضَ الجنرالُ

وقالَ لسيّافِهِ

أنْ يُعَدِّلَ ميلَ الوزيرِ

– على شاشةِ العرضِ –

قبلَ انتهاءِ المذيعةِ من طيِّ نشرتِها

ثمَّ اطوِ المذيعةَ

تحتَكَ

أو انشرِ الأرضَ شاهدةً

بين قبرِ الوزيرِ

وبين الجماهيرِ...]... دوزنَها الخوفُ

فارتفعتْ كالمآذِنِ آذانُها، تتقرّى

خطى الجَزَماتِ

أمامَ السلالِمِ

....

....

....

أراهنَّ

يهبطنَ للنبعِ

يقطفنَ بيضَ النجومِ

ويجمعنَها في السلالِ

يُفتِّشُ قلبيَ بين المطاراتِ والدُرجِ

عن شَعرِها

غيمةً ضفرَتها وصيفاتُ بابلَ

38

As he got up to explain,

the General was angry

and told his hitman

to adjust the Minister's posture

        on screen

before the presenter finished folding her papers.

Then fold her

under you

or scatter the earth as an epitaph

      between the grave of the Minister

and the masses...] and fear fine-tuned them

so they pricked up their ears like minarets, listening furtively for

the tramp of boots

up ladders.

....

....

....

I see the girls

go down to the spring

  to gather stars' eggs,

      collecting them in baskets.

    My heart searches between drawers and airports

for her hair

– clouds braided by Babylonian girls –

قبلَ دخولِ السبايا

– إلى قصرِهِ –

من عظامٍ تلامعُ في الشمسِ

أبوابُهُ من جلودٍ مدبَّغةٍ حينَ يفتحُها

ستئنُّ

فيرتعبُ الجنرالُ:

أوقفوا بفمِ الريحِ هذا الأنينَ]

أرى عينَ شمسي تجلَّتْ بوحدتِها

في عيوني

فكيف ألمَكِ في أعينِ الناظرين

بحُبِّكِ أخفاني الحُبُّ عنّي[18]

فكيف أُحِبُّ!؟

أريدُ من العشقِ هذا الفضاءَ الذي سوفَ يفتحُهُ لوزُ صدرِكِ

أذكرُ رائحةَ العُشْبِ في إبطيكِ

وأثملُ من عَرقٍ مشمشيٍّ

تحدَّرَ تحتَ قميصِكِ

في سَورةِ الوجدِ...

. . . .

. . . .

. . . .

يكفي قليلٌ من الناي كي تسكري بدموعي

ويكفي قليلٌ من الخمرِ والخبزِ كيما أُغنِّي...

على سُورِ معبدِ ننماخ[19]

ينفخُ ساحرُ مردوخ[20] ريشتَهُ

فيَشُقُّ الفضاءَ

40

before bringing the captive

to his palace of bones

shining in the sun,

his tanned leather gates creak

                when he opens them.

The General, frightened:

Stop this whingeing in the mouth of the wind.

I see the divine eye of Shamsy appear

                in my eye.

How can I protect you from the gaze of others?

I disappeared inside your love,[18]

            so how can I love?

I need from love a space, opened by the almonds of your breast.

I remember the smell of grass in your armpits

as I drank the apricot sweat

trickling under your shirt

in a blaze of passion.

     ....

     ....

     ....

     Enough of the flute will make you drunk on my tears.

        Enough wine and bread, and I will sing for you…

at the gates of Nanmakh's[19] temple

Marduk[20] the sorcerer blows on his quill

and parts the sky

باسْمي واسْمِكِ

ملتصِقَين

– على لوحةِ الأفقِ –

قوساً من اللازورد[21]

فتغضبُ جونو وتأمرُ حرّاسَها المترامينَ

أنْ يمْسكوا عنقَ الريحِ

يضحكُ منها تايريسياسُ: لا حبَّ يُدفنُ

تدفنُهُ في العراءِ إلى النصفِ،

تاركةً

عضــوَهُ

للكلابِ المجيعةِ

لكنَّ بعضَ اللصوصِ أزالوا الحروفَ

عن السُورِ،

كي يستدلّوا

على الكنزِ

لمْ يجدوا غيرَ فأرٍ عجوزٍ

طوى ذيلَهُ باتجاهِ الخزانةِ

يقرضُ ملحمةَ الطوفان

ركضنا إلى الثقْبِ كي نوقفَ الفيضان

فأوقفنا حارسُ المتحفِ البابليِّ:

– الزيارةُ ممنوعةٌ..

....

....

....

in my name and yours;

attached

to the skyline

is the arch of lazord[21]

where Juno rages, ordering her scattered guards

to grab the wind by the scruff of its neck.

Tireseus laughs: love cannot be buried,

yet Juno buries it out in the wasteland,

leaving it half-covered,

its penis exposed

to the starving dogs.

Some thieves swiped letters

from the wall

to lead them to

treasure

but they found only an old rat

that flicked its tail in the direction of the hoard

as it gnawed the flood epic.

We ran to help stem the flood

but the guard at the Museum of Babylon stopped us with

– *Visits are prohibited.*

....

....

....

هل ينقضي يومُنا في الجريدةِ؟

منغلقاً كالكتابِ،

أهدهدُ عينيكِ إذْ تنعسان

فتزلقُني فوقَ منحدرِ الصدرِ

يندلعُ الثدي من ثوبِها

نافراً

كغزالٍ شريدٍ

(- تناثرتُ فوقَ الأسرةِ

أيُّ سريرٍ يُدفِّئُني غيرُ هذي الأصابعِ مقرورةٍ

أتبطّنُها

وأنامُ؟) تُقلّبني النظراتُ

وتتركُني في الرفوفِ وحيداً، ألمُّ تقاطيعَها

عن مرايا الشوارعِ

لكنَّها إنْكَسَرَتْ

فتناثرتُ

(-كانَ حزيناً يمرُّ

أطالعُ عينيهِ منفتحاً كالكتابِ[22]

يحاورُني في السياسةِ

حتى إذا ما تعبنا غفا فوقَ زنديَّ

مبتهلاً

أنْ تَمُرَّ الغيومُ على وطني

بجعاً طائراً

يعبرُ الناي خصري، فيلتفُّ بي مثلَ لبلابةٍ

حالِماً بالقرى والمواويلِ في صالةِ الروك

حيثُ تطيرُ الموائدُ

مثلَ الغرانيقِ بيضاء

يتبعُها الندلُ مندهشين

Should we waste our days at the newspaper?

I am closed like a book.

I stroke your eyes as you drowse.

And she makes me slide between her breasts

as her breast bursts out of her dress

     free

       as a runaway ghazal

(– scattered over many beds,

which one will warm my body except these chilly fingers

which I clasp

as I sleep?) Many eyes scan me

    and leave me on the shelf, lonely, collecting her shape

      from street mirrors

but broken

and shattered.

(– He was sad when he walked past.

    I read his eyes like an open book.)[22]

He discussed politics with me

until we were tired, and he fell asleep on my arm

praying

the clouds over my country would pass

         like swans;

the flute across my waist, entwines me like ivy

I dream of villages and *mawawels* in a rock stadium

while tables are flying

   like white storks

     followed by astonished waiters

وتضحكُ

في عقدِها الخامسِ امرأةٌ تتصابى

يتعتعُها السُكْرُ:

هل سنطيرُ، أنا وحبيبي؟)

....

....

....

لا مراسٍ لنا: سفنٌ تشحنُ الذكرياتِ

وتمضي،

فأدنو من البحرِ، ألمسُ هذا التلاشي الشفيفَ

على زرقةِ الأفقِ:

كيف نصعتَ إلى حدِّ دمعي.

أأسرفتُ في الصحو؟

هلْ ينبغي أنْ يؤرجحَ رقَّاصُ أحلامِنا عمرَنا

لنقولَ تعبنا

فنَقْضِمُ نزْواتِنا

في الوسائدِ

أو مثلما تَقْضِمُ الإسطبلَ الخيولُ

إذا جوَّعتها السهولُ لأُحصي الذي ظلَّ لي

في الهوامشِ:

زقّورةً لا تُرَتِّبُ طابوقَها،

جملاً لمديحِ الأنوناكي[23]،

غاضبةً من أدابا وقلبي المصفَّدِ في الأيكيكي[24]،

أُريدُ

خريفاً

46

and she giggles

      childishly, a fifty year old woman

            staggering drunk,

     Are we going to fly, me and my darling?

....

....

....

We have no anchors, just ships that steal our memories

                            and sail away.

I come close to the sea, I touch the fading transparency

of the blue horizon.

    How did you shine like my tears?

Did I spend too long awake?

Must we be swung by the pendulum of our dreams, by our age?

                     So we say we are too tired

and bite our fantasies

into our pillow.

   As horses chew the stable

      if the fields make them hungry, I count what remains of me

in footnotes:

      a ziggurat that doesn't organise its bricks

            into sentences to praise the Anunnaki[23]

angry about Adab – and my heart that's handcuffed to the Ikeeki.[24]

    I want

      an autumn

لأُنضِجَ

هذا

النشيجَ،

نشيداً لـ أوروك

يختصرُ

الأرضَ

أبعدَ ما يبسطُ الشعراءُ الخيولَ

على السهلِ

والكتبِ المدرسيّةِ

لي أن أديرَ رَحَى الكلماتِ

وأطحنَ روحي لتشربَ قهوتَها في الصباحِ فتاةٌ

ترى غيرَ زرقةِ هذي السماء سماءً لعينيكِ لامعتين

وراءَ حديدِ السجونِ – الأغاني الشجيّةِ.

نشقى لأنَّ القصائدَ أبقى..

....

....

....

أعرفُ:

(ليلُ الطغاةِ طويلٌ) كما سيقولُ الرواةُ،...

(وعمري قصيرٌ) كما أخبرتني الحياةُ

فكيفَ أرى الفجرَ..

مِنْ أينَ يطلعُ

فجرُ العراقِ

                    to ripen

                        this

                        whimper

        into an anthem to Uruk

                that is the sum

                        of the earth.

        Beyond, poets spread horses

                over the fields

                and school books.

It's for me to turn the millstone of words

to grind my soul for a girl drinking coffee in the morning,

to see other than the blue of this sky, a sky for your shining eyes

            behind the iron of prisons and melancholy songs.

We suffer because poems last forever.

....

....

....

        I know

(the night of tyrants is long) as the storytellers told me

        (and my years are short) as life told me –

so how can I see the dawn?

How do we know where

        the dawn of Iraq rises

وحرّاسُنا

– كلَّ يومٍ –

يعلّون

أسوارَنا؟] ومن أينَ تأتين؟ ما بيننا العمرُ، هذي المفازاتُ،

والعَسَسُ المترامون وُسعَ المدى.

هل أرى ما ترى أو أرى نسغَ أمّي

يدبُّ من الأرضِ نحوَ الغصونِ الوريقةِ

هل تُزْهِرُ الأرضُ من دمعةٍ

سوف نسكبُها عابرين

إلى آخرِ النأي

نَحْمِلُ حصرانَنا وطناً

سوف نطويه في عجلٍ

كلّما داهمتنا المفارزُ...

نرحلُ في عضلٍ سائبٍ وحصانٍ رعى الشوكرانَ وماتَ

ليلهثَ في رئتي قمرٌ،

رافعاً ظلَّ ابهامِهِ تحتَ ضلعِ المساءِ...

عن النائمين وقوفاً بمخفرٍ كركوك

وهو يگزگزُ أسنانَهُ، كلّما جمعوا كتبَهُ

ورموها

ببابِ

المراحيضِ

يغمسُ أقدامَهُ بالمحابرِ

والدمِ

ثمَّ يهرولُ فوقَ السطورِ،

ليكتُبَ

تاريخَ أوروك

when the guards

    every day

        raise the fences?

            And how can you reach me when between us, life, distance

and policemen are spread out as far as the horizon?

Do I see what you see or do I see the essence of my mother creeping

from the earth towards the leafy branches.

Does the ground flower from a tear

        that we shed while passing through

                to the end of our journey?

We carry our mats like a country

and fold them quickly

whenever the security forces raid us...

We leave with wasted muscles and a horse grazing on hemlock that died.

So the moon breathed heavily into my lungs,

lifting the shadow of his thumb under the ribs of evening...

        About those who sleep standing up in Kirkuk police station

while he grinds his teeth: every time they pick up his books

                and throw them

                at the toilet

                door

he dips his feet into ink

        and blood

and hurries over the lines

to write

the history of Uruk.

....
....
....

تقفزُ أيَّامُهُ كالبراغيثِ، فوقَ يديهِ

فيفقسُها

ويحكُّ الحديدَ بأظفارِهِ

كي يدمِّي منافيهِ،

لكنَّهم سحبوا في السجونِ أظافرَهُ،

فنمتْ – في أناملِهِ العشرِ – عشرُ زنابق

[أمسحُ عن مقلتيكِ ظلالَ المآذنِ،

كي تُبصِري الآن هذي السماءَ الوسيعةَ

لي زعترٌ ناضجٌ في خسائرِ حقلي،

ويضحكُ دِعْبلُ

من عانةِ المتوكِّل

ينتفُها

الترك

في البركةِ الزئبقيَّةِ

أفتحُ قلبي لأمسحَ عنه غبارَ الملوكِ

وقيحَ الشكوكِ

لهم أنْ يذرّوا

الرمادَ

.. بعامِ الرَمَادةِ[25]،

كي لا نرى سارقَ الجهرِ

يَقْطَعُ

في سارقِ السِرِّ[26]

....
....
....

His days are leaping like fleas on his hands

        so he hatches them −

scratches the iron bars with his fingernails

        in order to bleed his exile.

But in prison, they pulled out his fingernails

    so ten lilies grew on his ten fingers

      (wipe the shadows of the minarets from your eyes

        so you can see this wide sky).

I have ripe thyme in my lost field

       and Dabal laughs

          at Al-Mutawakkil's groin

plucked by

the Turks

in a pool of mercury.

I open my heart to wipe from it the dust of kings

       and the pus of doubts.

They scatter the

    ashes

    in Aam Alramada[25]

so as not to see the public thief

cut off

the hand of the secret thief.[26]

....

....

....

نغرسُ أسنانَنا في الهواءِ، نشيِّدُ زقّورةً في

عراءِ الحضاراتِ [عَبُّودُ قال: الحضارةُ جنسٌ وليستْ جناسٌ...

ويضحكُ إذْ يتذكّرُ

كيفَ تلعثمَ – في المسرحِ البابليِّ –

الدليلُ السياحيُّ حين رأى في ظلالِ المُدرَّجِ سروالَ سائحةٍ

تَجلِسُ القرفصاءَ...]

يجيءُ المغولُ على خيلِنا الضامرات

تخوّضُ في دِمِنا: أزرقاً كالمحابرِ أو أحمراً في المحاجرِ

تأتي المدافعُ

يأتي الوشاةُ

فتنسلُّ جندرمةُ الانكليز إلى بيتِ شعلان[27]

تأتي جيوشُ أُميّة من سُورةِ الفتحِ[28]

....

....

....

أشيرُ إلى الأفقِ أسودَ من ذَرَقِ الطائراتِ

يقهقهُ عَبُّودُ وهو يشيرُ إلى ثقْبِ سترتِه:

من هنا مرَّتِ الحربُ...

....

....

....

54

....
....
....

We plant our teeth in the air, we build ziggurats in the nakedness
of the ages (Aboud said: *Civilisation is sex, not alliteration...*
and he laughs when he remembers
how he stuttered in the Babylonian theatre –
when the tour guide saw a tourist perched on the steps of the arena
    and he glimpsed her knickers).
    The Mongols come, riding our skinny horses
bursting into our blood that's blue as ink or red as a bloodshot eye.
    First come cannons
        then informers
            then British soldiers who tiptoe into Sha'lān's house[27]
as the Umayyad armies evacuate Sūrat al-Fath[28]...

....
....
....

I point to the horizon, black with aircraft droppings
and Aboud guffaws while showing off the hole in his jacket
where the war went through...

....
....
....

55

أرى في البروقِ الغبوقَ الذي يترقرقُ

في جفنِ عشتار[29]...

لكنَّني لا أرى في البحارِ سوى

ما يردُّ الغريبَ إلى أهلِهِ:

جُثَّةً

أو صناديقَ مختومةً هائماً في العبابِ

... غنيمته بالإيابِ

ليصحو على ظلِّ ايقونةٍ

وفتاةٍ من القَشِّ

لا تُتقِنُ الحبَّ إلَّا ببابِ المطابخ

....

....

....

أقولُ للوركا: بأنكِ بيضاءُ أكثرَ من دمعِ صاريةٍ خارجَ البحرِ،

زرقاءَ كالروحِ عطَّشَها الحبُّ والحربُ،

خضراءَ من سُكَّرٍ وظلالٍ. وقرطبة من دموعٍ وماسٍ.

أقولُ لناظم: يالفراقِكِ من مهنةٍ شاقةٍ[30].

وأقولُ لصحبي: اشريوني على مَهَلٍ

لتذوقوا حلاوةَ روحي،

ولا تَكْسِروا الكَأسَ

في القطراتِ الأخيرةِ

يعتقُ خمري

أنا دمعةٌ أطلقتها عيونُ الأميرِ المُودِّعِ غرناطةً،

سُرقتْ قبلَ أن تصلَّ الأرضَ.

56

I see lightning flicker

        under Ishtar's eyelids[29]

but in the sea, I only catch sight of

what a stranger returns to his family:

            a corpse

or stamped boxes lost in the torrent

…his reward is to return,

for them to wake up to the shadow of an icon

      and a girl made of straw

         who only knows love at the kitchen door.

…………………………

…………………………

…………………………

I say to Lorca: *She is whiter than a sail on the sea,*

blue like a spirit thirsty from love and war,

green from honey and shadows and the Cordoba of tears and diamonds.

I tell Nazim Hikmet: *Separation is a hard path* [30]

and I tell my friends: *Drink me slowly*

      to taste the sweetness of my soul,

       without breaking the glass –

for in the last drop

      is my maturity.

I'm the tear shed by the prince's eye when he left Granada,

stolen before reaching the ground.

من ألفِ عامٍ ولا أصلُ الأرضَ.

في جسدي طعناتُ القبائلِ تمضي

إلى الغزوِ والتكنولوجيا.

أفرُّ من اسمي وأختارُ نزلاً بضاحيةٍ

لا تساومُ أزهارُها رئتي،

لا غرابٌ يُقلّدُ زقزقتي.

أمهرُ الكائناتِ بوسمي ليُنكِرَني فرسي

فوقَ جلدِ العبارةِ، رمحي سيأكلُهُ العثُّ.

أسقُطُ.

سهواً تجيءُ الحضارات،

سهواً تجيءُ الملوكُ

وسهواً نجيءُ

فمَنْ قسَّمَ الأرضَ ما بيننا:

فلهم قمحُها

ولنا قَحْطُها

ولهم نفطُها

ولنا لغطُها

....

....

....

هل المُلْكُ يملكُ تبريرَهُ...

كلَّما سفحوا دمَنا في الحروبِ

نما زهرُ تيجانِهم في السهوبِ

أريدُ هواءً يُترجِمُني في نصوصِ التشابكِ بيني

For one thousand years, I'm not reaching the ground.

In my body the stabs of the tribes have progressed

to invasion and technology.

> I escape from my name and choose a small house in the suburbs
>
> where the flowers don't bargain with my lungs
>
> and crows can't mimic my harmonies.
>
> I stamp creatures with my mark, so my horse doesn't know me
>
> over a skin of phrases. The mites will eat my spear.

I fell.

Inadvertently, civilisations come.

Inadvertently, kings come.

> Inadvertently, we have come

who divided the earth between us:

> they have wheat
>
> we have drought
>
> > they have oil
> >
> > we have clamour.

. . . .

. . . .

. . . .

Do our owners have any excuse

> when they shed our blood in wars
>
> > and their crowns flourish like flowers in the field?

I want air that interprets *me* in the tangled texts between me

وبين القصيدةِ مبحوحة الصوتِ
من فرطِ ما صرختْ في الخنادقِ،
ملتصقاً بالمعا – يا ابن عمسل[31] –
لمْ أُدَّخرْ فضلةَ الزادِ إلَّا تعلَّةً
هذا الزمانِ الذي [أقبلتْ كقطيعٍ من الليلِ هذي المفاتنُ[32] –
هذا الزمانُ:

قلوبٌ اليكَ،

سيوفٌ عليكَ[33]

فكيف تُفرِّقُ بينهما
حين تشتبكُ الخيلُ بالخيلِ
والليلُ بالليلِ]
لِ
لِ
لِ، لِ، لِ،

....

....

....

أسمعُ قرقعةَ الواجهاتِ، النصوصِ، سحاقِ الزجاجِ بأضراسِنا،
من أخاديدِها يهربُ الدودُ لحظةَ تمشي المقابرُ
– أقْصِدُ – تمشي المعاجمُ
نحوَ المدينةِ جمعَ عظايا، هياكلَ ممطوطةً،
يهربُ الناسُ، أعمدةُ الكهرباء، الدروبُ، المزارعُ، والمركباتُ
صحوتُ على صوتِ سيَّارةِ إسعاف
تحملُ وعيي
إلى صالةِ العمليَّاتِ،

60

and the voice of poetry that's hoarse

because of the long time I've been yelling in the trenches,

sticking out my stomach – *O, son of Emsal*[31]–

I didn't save much food, only barely enough to survive starvation,

this era arrived like a herd of the night, showing its charms.[32]

This age is –

         hearts with you

             swords against you,[33]

how can you differentiate between them

    when horses are mingled with horses

and night with night

        ı

        t

        ttt

    ....

    ....

    ....

I hear the rattle of shop fronts, texts, and the crack of teeth against glass:

worms wriggle from potholes the moment graveyards

– I mean skeletons – start to

    walk towards the city, issuing commands: the skeletons reach out:

people run away, so do electricity pylons, roads, farms and vans....

I wake to the sound of an ambulance

        carrying my mind

        to the operating room,

مختنقاً بغبارِ القواميسِ والستراتِ.
يهرولُ مَصْلي بأنبوبةِ الطرقاتِ
إلى البحرِ

أفتحُ عيني على البحرِ
كان جهازُ ECG عاطلاً، والستائرُ مسدلةً،
والأطباءُ منكفئينَ على جُثَّتي
بالمشارطِ
صحتُ: اتركوني أقصُّ لكم ما رأيتُ...
فلمْ يمنحوني انتباهاً
وراحَ الخبيرُ يُفصِّلُني – فوقَ مَشْرَحَةِ النَّصِّ –
منشغلاً بتلاميذِهِ
فأسدلتُ جفني ونمتُ عميقاً...

رأيتُ الكواكبَ تسجدُ لي
والقيامةَ ذاتَ البروقِ تضجُّ بحشدِ العَرايا
تفوحُ بسيلِ الخطايا...
واسرافيلَ ينفخُ في بوقِهِ:
انهضوا يا نيامَ القرونِ الكسيحةِ...
صحتُ: أينَ الإلهُ؟

فهبَّ الغبارُ يُغَطِّي الوجوةَ التي نهضتْ في بجاماتِها فزعاً...
وتمطَّى الإلهُ يُقلِّبُ دفتريَ الضخمَ...
تلكَ حياتي إذاً؟
راكضاً في الجحيمِ أولولُ:
أينَ ذنوبُ الطغاة؟
فامسكني نادلُ البارِ:
صَهْ

choked by the dust of dictionaries and nurses.

And my serum runs away down a tube of streets

to the sea...

And I opened my eyes to the sea.

The ECG machine was faulty, the curtains drawn,

the surgeons gathered round my body

with scalpels.

I shouted: *Let me tell you what I saw...!*

but they wouldn't listen

and the professor began cutting me – over a morgue of text –

busy with his students,

so I closed my eyes and slept deeply.

I saw the planets kneeling to me

and the resurrection, ablaze with lightning, crammed with naked crowds

overflowing with their mistakes...

and Israfil blew his horn:

Wake up you sleeping people from your crippled centuries!

I shouted: *Where is God?*

Dust settled on their faces when they woke, terrified, in their pyjamas...

and God stretched himself and flicked through my thick book.

So this is my life?

Running in hell screaming:

Where are the sins of the tyrants?

The bartender grabbed me:

Quiet!

....

....

....

غَطَّيتُ رأسي بملحفةِ السجنِ مملوءةٍ بالصراخاتِ والقملِ

نمتُ عميقاً

رأيتُ الثُرَيّا التي تتلامعُ في كبدِ الليلِ

تدنو...

تحطُّ على كوّتي

كيف أقطفُها ويدايَ مكبّلتانِ

إلى عنقي

....

....

....

أيُّها...

... الجنرالُ

الذي كانَ يرقبُ

– من شاشةٍ قربَ مضجعِهِ –

الراجماتِ تدكُّ مدائنَنا

وهو يَعْلُكُ غليونَهُ الأجنبيَّ:

أهذا إذاً كلُّ ما ظلَّ من وطني؟ (– أيّها الميتون قياماً:[34]

مشكولُ الذمةِ علّهُ الفالةُ[35]...

....

....

....

....

....

....

I covered my head with a prison blanket infested with lice and screams
and slept for a long time.
I saw the Pleiades shining in the dead of night,
coming closer
landing on my window sill.

   How can I pick them up while my hands are handcuffed
behind my neck?

....

....

....

O...
   General,
      monitoring
         from a screen next to his bed
            the mortars pounding our cities
         while chewing the stem of his foreign pipe,
is this all that's left of my homeland? (*Wake up you dead!* [34]
and *Please can I have my pitchfork back?*) [35]

....

....

....

خذْ دموعي

– إلى البحرِ –

يا شِعرُ

واغسلْ حجارتَها من غبارِ الطحالبِ،

جرَّتْ جرارَ سنيني إلى بذخِ الكائناتِ،

تسيلُ وتَكتُبُني في زفيرِ الكتابةِ

– هذا البهاء الذي يتكوكبُ

....

....

....

كاشيرةُ الحزبِ،

كانتْ تَعُدُّ ضلوعي

لتنقصَ من جسدي

شجراً مُورقاً

ثمَّ تُخْطِيءُ في العدِّ

أتركُ سُخريَّتي مُرَّةً

وأذوَّبُ في قهوتي

ضحكَ الفتياتِ على سائقِ الباصِ

وهو يُمَشِّطُ أجسادَهنَّ بنظراتِهِ

تحتَ شمسِ السلامِ الرخيّةِ

أرنو لعابرةٍ

تركْتْ – في فضاءِ البنفسج – نظرتَها

لتسلّمَ روحي مفاتيحَها للغروبِ

كلامي يضيئُكَ

يا أورفيوسُ، المُحلّقُ:

O poetry,

      take my tears

            to the sea

      and wash their stones free from the dust of seaweed;

      from the tarnished urn in which I'm displayed to the creatures

      of the universe I leak out in words

      as an exhalation of glory turned into stars…

      …………………………

      …………………………

      …………………………

The treasurer of the political party

      was counting my ribs

         to deduct them from my body

            like saplings.

Then she does a miscount

and I abandon my bitter sarcasm

and stir into my coffee

the giggling of some girls about their bus driver

            (who is combing their bodies with his eyes)

                    under the soft sun of peace.

I look closely at a woman passerby –

      she leaves her gaze in a purple space

         so my soul gives its keys to the sunset.

My words light you,

      O rising Orpheus,

لا تلتفتْ لخرابِ البلادِ
التي كنتَ ودَّعتها في الأفولِ على مضضٍ،
عاكفاً بالتماسِ هشيمي على نهرِ ايدسالا.

أنا، كلَّما مرَّتِ الطائراتُ
انحنيتُ على وطني وبكيتُ.
مسرَّدةٌ أضلعي في الكماناتِ.
أبني على الرملِ بيتاً
وأهدمُهُ.
ثمَّ أهرمُ كالبيتِ في راحةِ اليدِ.
تغفو القنابلُ
فوقَ وسائدِنا الحجريَّةِ،
وهو يكشّطُ تاريخَهُ:
حرشفاً من سلالاتِهِ، فيرى صوراً نَشَّفُوا ريقَها
من مداهمةِ الشرطةِ. العرباتُ تجرُّ السوادَ
إلى شجري، مدداً آسناً تحتويه الفنادقُ حتى
تُطلَّ بشبّاكِهِ رجفةُ القذفِ في صورِ البطلاتِ الخليعاتِ.
لا تلتفتْ للوراءِ،
فماضيك قبرُكَ
كانَ يجوبُ المطاراتِ من دونِ أنْ يتركَ شبّاكَهُ
لحظةً، هائماً في البلادِ وأحزانُهُ تَجلِسُ القرفصاءَ
بسجنِ أبي غريب
ترنو إلى كلِّ مَنْ أُعدموا
قبلَ أنْ ينطقوا

....
....
....

68

don't look back at the ruins of the country

  you said goodbye to, in an ending, reluctantly;

  focus on seeking my wreckage on the river Idsala.

Each time a plane passes

  I bow to my country and cry.

My ribs diffuse over the violins.

I build a house on sand

  and destroy it,

then I age like a house in the palm of the hand.

The bombs sleep

on top of our stone pillows,

and he peels off the scales of his history

      from his descendants and sees photos that dry his saliva

      like a police raid. The lorries pull darkness

   towards my trees, a stagnant waste by the hotels and a

   shivering ejaculation, watching porn stars out of his window.

  Don't look back,

      for your past is your tomb.

He used to travel through airports without leaving his window for a

moment, hanging around in his country, his despair sitting like a squatter

      in Abu Ghraib prison,

gazing at all those executed

  before they had a chance to speak.

. . . .

. . . .

. . . .

أسمعُ خشخشةَ القيدِ في كفِّ عَبُّود

يشطبُ يوماً بتقويم مايا هوغا[36]

ويرفعُ أظفارَهُ للسماءِ،

ليخمشَ وجةَ الإلهِ

فينهرُهُ رجلُ الدينِ

يحملُ مِسبَحَةً طولها... (- لا يجوزُ

مقايسةَ

العضوِ)

.. ترنو إليه الفتاةُ التي [اكتملَ البدرُ

في صدرِها

سوف ترنو لمرآتِها

وهي تفتحُ أزرارَ غاباتِها

تتأفَّفُ من ضجرِ العطلةِ المدرسيَّةِ.

تأتي صديقتُها، ستقولُ لها أنَّ هذا الكمثرى، على الصدرِ،

يُوجِعُها

فتمسِّدُهُ باشتهاءٍ خفيٍّ

تفكُّ عن البحرِ شطآنَهُ

تنتشي البنتُ

تُصغي لصوتِ هديلِ الحَمَامِ يُنقِّرُ في كرزِها،

ناعماً،

ويطيرُ،

فتنزلُ نحوَ اللجينِ،

تهدّجُ محمومةَ الهمسِ،

حالِمةً بالمراكبِ، تشبكُها وتشبّانِ كالموجِ،

يعلو ويهبطُ...

حين تهمّانِ...] تزعقُ

70

I hear the sound of the handcuffs on Aboud's wrists

    ticking off a day on the Hindu calendar[36]

        and raising his fingernails to the sky

            to scratch God's face

for which he gets reprimanded by the clergyman

    holding a rosary, it's very long (− don't

            measure

            the penis!)

The girl − with a chest like a full moon −

            winks at him

and looks in her mirror

while opening the secrets of her forests

complaining about holiday boredom.

    Her friend comes, and she tells her the pear on her chest

    hurts her

        she touches it gently in secret lust

that releases the sea from its shores.

The girl gets excited

listening to the cooing of a pigeon, pecking at her berry

        softly

          and flying away.

    Then she goes down into the silvery waves

whispering in a fevered whisper,

dreaming of boats, they hug and rise like the swell,

rising and falling.

When they start, the warning siren

صافرةٌ في سماءِ المدينةِ

تهرعُ نحوَ الملاجيءِ

يمْسِكُها رجلُ الدينِ من ردنِها،

راكضاً:

لا يجوزُ ملامسةَ العضوِ...

رأيتُ إلى الشلمغانيِّ[37]، فوقَ الصليبِ

ينادي ببّكةً:

– لا عقدَ بين الفروجِ

....

....

....

هل يخسرُ البحرُ أمواجَهُ،

مثلما يخسرُ القلبُ أحراشَهُ في الصداقاتِ؟

هل بدأ الكونُ

من قبّةٍ في العماءِ؟

تطوفُ

على الماءِ،

رجراجةً في الظلاماتِ

من رعشةِ الخصبِ في عضوِ أبسو

يدبُ ببطنِ تيامت[38]،

نابضةً بالمكائدِ والخبزِ..

هل كان في بطنِها الغيمُ ينمو، كما الشهواتُ

فتلبطُ أسماكُها الكوكبيّةُ في النطفةِ الأزليّةِ

72

screams in the city sky.

She runs to the shelters,

the priest grabs her by her sleeve,

       running...

       Genitals mustn't be touched!

I saw Shalmaghani[37] on the cross

shouting in Mecca

– *Genitals don't need a marriage contract.*

....
....
....

Does the ocean lose its waves,

      like the heart sheds its leaves through friendships?

Did the universe start

     from an arch of blindness?

Floating

on the water,

a sway in the dark

from a spasm in Abzû's penis

crawls into Tiamat's[38] belly

pulsing with yeast and schemes.

Did these clouds of trickery grow in her belly, like lust,

as the sperm swam towards the egg?

فانبثقتْ هذه الأرضُ من قطرةٍ حائزةٍ في التهدّجِ، سهواً، يباركُها لوحُ مموٍ[39] بِبلبالةٍ. فاذا هدأتْ شقشقاتُ العناقِ الإلهيِّ بينهما، سحبتْ بطنَها المتثاقلَ فوقَ الضفافِ وخيطاً من الدمِ يسبحُ في الطميِّ...

هل كان لخمو يمازجُ روحَ لخامو[40]

على شرشفِ الأفقِ المخمليِّ

فينشر أنشارُ أمواجَهُ كالسديمِ

وتهبطُ كيشارُ بين الشعابِ[41]

وبين اختلاطِهما وافتراقِهما انحسرتْ في السباتِ السماءُ

عن الربِّ آنو وكّي

فكان إيا سيِّد الأرضِ[42]

ينفخُ مبتهجاً بمزاميرِه

ليهندسَ في روحِهِ الكائناتِ الجميلةَ

حتى إذا ابتهجوا في البلادِ

وضجَّتْ دفوفُ الحصادِ

على الأرضِ

هدّهمُ طوفانُ المياهِ...

الجرادُ...

الطواغيتُ..

ماذا صنعتَ بنا أيُّها الجنرالُ المُولَّهُ بالتيهِ؟

ماذا فعلتَ بهذي البلادِ

التي لم تجدْ شجراً تتوكَّأُهُ، غيرَ سيفِكَ

أو مطراً تستقي زرعَها

غيرَ

بولِكَ

من تحتِ أنقاضِ عصرِ الطواغيتِ،

The land emerged in religious ecstasy, casually from a hot drop blessed
by Mamu's[39] tablet. In between the god's embraces she dragged her
heavy belly across the banks, and a thread of blood swam in the mud…
Does Lahmu mix with the soul of Lahamu[40]

    on the sheets of the velvet horizon

   while Anshar spreads his waves like a haze

     and Kishar drops between the corals.[41]

  Between their mingling and parting the sky faded

    from Anu and Kai into sleep –

Aya ruled the earth[42]

  eagerly blowing her horn

to make everything in her being beautiful

and joyful in the land –

now harvest drums sound

  on the land

destroyed by the flood

    by locusts…

     by tyrants…

What have you done to us, O General who is passionate about mazes?
What did you do to this country?

  It can find no trees to lean on, other than your sword,

   and nothing to water it

    but

    your piss.

From under the ruins of the age of tyrants,

ينهضُ قلبي

يُغنّي...

لعاشقةٍ، رحلتْ كذبولِ قرنفلةٍ

فوق شطآنِ اينون

فانتحبَ الكورسُ:

أنساكَ شهدُ اللذاذاتِ، سهدَ التجاريبِ

لكنَّ روحيَ شوَّهها السجنُ

....

....

....

والعصرِ[43].

إنَّ الشعراءَ لَفي خُسرٍ،

إلّا النقَّارينَ على طبلٍ

والهزَّازينَ على حبلٍ

والماشينَ مع النهرِ

فاحرقْ أوراقَكَ، يا ابن الصائغِ،

لن تجنيَ من هذا العالمِ

غيرَ القهرِ.

وهذا الشعر يغلَفُ عينيكَ بمنديلِ الدمع

فلا تُبْصِرُ من متعِ الدنيا شيئاً.

واوٌ

طاءٌ

نونٌ..

مرَّ الحرّاسُ على جفني فاستوقفهم

وَقعُ خطىً ينسلُ خفيفاً بين الأهدابِ وبيني...

شرعوا ببنادقِهم

76

my heart rises

        singing...

    for a lover, that's left like a wilting carnation

    on the shores of Aynoon.

The chorus wails:

The honey of desire makes you forget the sleeplessness of life's stresses.

But my soul has been deformed by prison.

....

....

....

I swear by time[43]

that poets are losers

unlike drummers

and opportunists

and people who go with the flow.

So burn your papers, Mister Al-Sayegh,

you won't get anything from this world

           except depression.

    This poetry is covering your eyes with a cloth of tears

    so you don't see any of the world's joys

na

  ti

    on

The guards walked over my eyelids and were stopped by

the sound of footsteps sneaking between my eyebrows and me...

they cocked their rifles

صفاً صفاً

وانتظروا...

فصرختُ بهم:

هذا قلبي!...

يا هذا الملفوفُ بأوراقِ الآسِ،

لماذا تتركُ حجرَتَكَ البلَّوْريَّةَ كي تتسكَّعُ في الطرقاتِ المحظورةِ..

(قلتُ سأختصرُ العمرَ الفضفاضَ،

بسطرين يتيمين من الشِعرِ،

على قبرٍ مجهولٍ.

وأريحُ العالَم

من ثرثرةِ الشعراءِ.

سأختصرُ القلبَ على نهديْ امرأةٍ يكتظَّانِ بشوقٍ مسعورٍ

تحتَ قميصِ الشيفونِ الشفافِ،

وأمضي) مرتعشَ الأحلامِ

يطاردُني أفقٌ من غيمٍ ونباحٍ

يتكاثفُ فوقَ زجاجي مطراً أسودَ...

فالليلةَ لا تعصمُني من طوفانِ الحزنِ الممتدِّ

جبالُ الكلماتِ، ولا...

أحرقُها وأذرُّ رمادَ الحلّاجِ المصلوبِ

على عينِ الزمنِ الأعْورِ (في صدري قنبلةٌ من قيحٍ

ويناقشُني كاظمُ عَبْدُ[44] عن الشِعرِ الرومانسيِّ

صباحَ الخيرِ، الشعراءَ السبعينيين، التسعينيين، بمقهى العجميِّ، يُفَلّون قصائدَ

بعضِهم البعض ويختصمونَ على المبنى.

قلتُ: صباحَ الخيرِ، وما ردَّ سوى النادلِ.

لا وقتَ لعمري المتسارعِ أن يَجلِسَ في المقهى، فالفوَّهةُ الملعونةُ

ما زالتْ تترصَّدُني

خلفَ الصخرةِ.

78

line by line

    and they waited...

I shouted at them

This is my heart,

you who are covered with myrtle leaves,

why would you leave your crystal room to loiter along forbidden roads?

− I said *I shall reduce this overflowing life*

    into two orphaned lines of verse

        on an unknown grave

and go from the world

    and the babble of poetry.

I will squeeze my heart between a woman's breasts, eager

    under a transparent chiffon blouse,

        and walk away shivering with dreams

        haunted by horizons of clouds and barking,

condensing like black rain over my window.

Night doesn't protect me from the flood of sadness

as mountains of words don't, and I don't...

I burn it and scatter the ashes of the crucified Al-Halaj

over one-eyed history (in my heart there is a bomb of pus

and Kadhim Abed[44] arguing about romantic poetry).

    Good morning seventies poets, nineties poets, in the Ajmi

coffee shop, unravelling each other's poetry and disputing the form;

    I said, good morning, but only the waiter replied.

My life is disappearing too fast to sit in a café with that damn muzzle

still lurking

    behind a rock.

قلتُ لأعبرَ نهرَ الخوفِ المُتعرِّجَ نحوَ...

وأحجمتُ

فعينُ القنَّاصِ الأعورِ لا ترحمُ أحلامَ الشعراءِ...

(ولا بأسَ سأجلسُ بين الأحجارِ أو الكلماتِ،

أعدُّ بكلِّ هدوءٍ أوراقَ الأيّامِ على ضوءِ الفانوسِ،

فأُبصِرُها شاحبةً تتساقطُ...

تحطبُها الحربُ على عجلٍ، لتُدفِّئَ أحلامَ المدنِ المقرورةِ)

يا طينَ النهرِ اللاصقِ في قدميَّ الحافيتين

سلاماً، يا سوباطَ طفولتِنا الحامضَ،

يا شجرَ التوتِ المائلَ نحوَ الجرفِ،

ألمْ تتعبْكَ مشاكسةُ الصبيانِ المختبئين

بلحيتِكَ البيضاء،

سلاماً، عينَ الجارةِ من شقِّ البابِ

سلاماً، سَبُوراتِ الدرسِ السوداءَ،

الدشداشاتِ المحشورةَ في البنطالِ، سلاماً، يا أقبيةَ التعذيبِ

(التلفازُ يوزِّعُ مجاناً نشراتِ الموتِ،

على روّادِ المقهى، والضجرَ اليوميَّ...

– ألا تشربُ شيئاً؟

ثمةَ فأرٌ يقرضُ حبلَ الجملةِ

– ما أخبارُ البصرةِ، يا ابنَ اللنكك؟[45]

ينقطعُ البثُّ فتَربِطُهُ بشريطِ أغاني النصرِ مذيعاتُ الربطِ،

ويتركنَ الشَعرَ المفلولَ بدونِ شرائطَ، منتثراً فوقَ وجوهِ الروّادِ

الملصوقةِ بالشاشةِ

مرّتْ أسرابُ الميغِ، وأصواتُ الباعةِ، والدومينو...

(– كأسُ هدوءٍ من فضلِكَ)

مرّتْ مفرزةُ الإعدامِ وأسرابُ الذبّانِ وعطرُ امرأةٍ عابرةٍ

(– أينَ الخُلّانُ؟ أهذا "زمنُ الصمتِ!؟

I said, *Let me cross the river of fear, zigzagging towards...*

and I stopped.

The eye of the one-eyed sniper shows no mercy to poets.

That's OK, I'll just sit between the rock and the words.

I leaf through the pages of my diary by lamplight;

I see them pale and falling, cut down hastily by the war

to warm the dreams of shivering cities –

the mud of the river stuck to my bare feet.

Hello to the sour grapes of our childhood,

weighing the tree down to the earth,

aren't you tired of boys hiding their mischief

behind your white beard?

Hello to the eye of the woman neighbour through the door crack.

Hello to the classroom blackboards,

the shirts tucked into our pants, the torture cells

(TV distributes free death updates

to the customers in the café) and the daily boredom.

Would you like something to drink?

A mouse is nibbling the sentence.

What news of Basra, O son of Al-Linkik? [45]

The programme breaks off for the announcer to introduce victory songs.

She reconnects the tape then unties her hair to spread across the faces

gawping at the TV screen.

MiG squadrons fly past a hubbub of street-sellers and domino-players

(*a glass of quiet please*)

the death squad, swarms of flies and the scent of a passing woman

(*Where are the friends? Is this the time of silence!?*

81

وملازمةُ البيتِ"!!؟)[46] اختلطتْ فوقَ ذهولِ زجاجِ المقهى

دقَّاتُ الطبلِ ورجعُ نساءٍ يعولنَ على جسرِ الجمهوريةِ

يقطعُهُ نَقْرُ دفوفٍ وصبايا

اختلطتْ رائحةُ الآسِ برائحةِ الحِنَّاءِ

الشمعُ

الطلقاتُ

اندفع اللغطُ المتراشقُ

ثمَّ انجابَ سريعاً عن قهقهةٍ في زاويةِ المقهى

فبكى الكهلُ المَحْنيُّ الظهر على الدنيا،

حتى بانَ النابُ الأوحدُ في فكَّيهِ

تحسَّستُ بقايا أسناني، ومضيتُ وحيداً

لي أحلامٌ أُبصِرُها تنقُصُ

كلَّ صباحٍ

– مَنْ يسرقُ أحلامي في الليلِ إذاً يا عَبُّودُ؟

صباحٌ بمزاجِ عصافيرٍ تَنقُرُ نافذةَ الروحِ

– أَأفتحُها؟

(– والقنَّاصُ؟)

ألا يتركُ لي مُتَّسَعاً لتأمُّلِ هذا الفجرِ الفيروزيِّ الأزرقِ مثل قميصٍ مراهقةٍ مفتوحٍ خلفَ الكثبانِ البيضِ.

يسيلُ لُعابُ الكلماتِ بحلقي المتشنِّج

من فرطِ الصمتِ وكبتِ السنواتِ المرَّةِ. لو يغسلُ

هذا المطرُ الناعمُ أحزانَ العالمِ في روحي

مطرٌ من ليمونٍ وأغانٍ

مطرٌ من فئرانٍ سودٍ

مطرٌ من خوذٍ وطبولٍ،

مطرٌ من شقراواتٍ يلعبنَ البوكرَ...

82

And staying at home!!?) [46] Behind the astonished coffee shop window,

drum beats mingle with women wailing on Al-Jumhory Bridge,

intercut by the sound of tambourines and girls,

    the fragrance of myrtle, henna,

        candles

        and bullets.

The clamour quickly faded,

drowned out by laughter from the corner of the café

and an old man hunched forward and cried for the world,

        showing his one tooth.

I checked the rest of my teeth and walked away alone.

I see my dreams diminishing

        every morning

– *Who steals my dreams in the night then, O Aboud?*

Morning is a mood of sparrows pecking at the window of my soul.

– *Should I open it?*

– *(And the sniper?)*

Will he not leave me a space to meditate in this turquoise blue dawn like

the open shirt of a young girl behind white dunes.

Words drip and play in my convulsing throat

from an excess of silence, from suppressing the bitter years. If only this

soft rain would wash the sadness of the world from my essence.

    Rain from lemons and songs.

        Rain from black rats.

            Rain from helmets and drums.

                Rain from blondes playing poker…

(محتضناً جمجمتي الزرقاءَ على مَشرحةِ العصرِ

تؤرِّخُ بالكدماتِ طفولتَنا المنسيَّةَ،

في حاناتِ القملِ، وأقبيةِ التعذيبِ.

نُعَلِّقُ فوقَ المسمارِ رئاتٍ ينخرُها الصرصرُ والحزنُ،

نُنفِّضُها في الصبحِ ونلبسُها عجلين.

مضى العمرُ بنفخةِ نارٍ...)[47]

وأصيحُ على قارعةِ المارّةِ:

— مَنْ يرحمُ عمراً كالثلجِ يذوبُ

بعزِّ الصيفِ؟[48]

بكيتُ على صحبٍ سيذوبونَ على طاولتي.

أحسستُ بلا جدوى العالمِ. مَنْ يدري قد تصبحُ آخرَ ما

أكتبُهُ هذي الهذياناتُ، وقد لا أُكمِلُها...

مَنْ يضمنُ عمراً

في ماسورةِ قنّاصٍ (رأسي ما زالَ يُواصِلُ مضغَ

حشيشِ الأفكارِ بمرعى النجماتِ. — متى أغفو؟

طالَ الليلُ كثيراً خلفَ القضبانِ، وهذا السَّجانُ الأزليُّ يسرقُ

من زيتِكَ يا وطني كلَّ مساءٍ قطرةَ ضوءٍ...)

آهٍ.. لو أتمدَّدُ في الليلِ الصيفيِّ المقمرِ فوقَ السطحِ المرشوشِ،

وأُصغي كالطفلِ لكلِّ حكايا أمي...

لولا تلكَ العينانِ الجامِدَتان

لأحصيتُ النجماتِ على السطحِ:

"كلا،... بالا،... برتقالا،...

عمي،... گلي،... جيب الكالا...

وي..."[49]

... أفتحُ علبةَ سردين.

أتمدَّدُ فيها،

وأنامُ

84

(Hugging my blue skull on the morgue of this age

noting history in the bruises of our forgotten childhood,

in the pubs of lice and the basements of torture.

We hang up on screws our lungs gnawed by cockroaches and sadness,

we shake them out in the morning and put them on quick.

Time passes with a breath of fire...)[47]

And I shout in the crowded street:

– *Who will have mercy on a life that melts like ice*

in the swelter of summer? [48]

I cried for friends who will melt on my table.

I felt that the world has no purpose. Who knows if the last thing I'll

write will be delusions, and maybe I won't complete them...

     Who guarantees life

          if a sniper has it in his sights? (My mind continues to chew

over the grass of thoughts in a field of stars – when will I fall asleep?

The night is long behind bars, and every evening the eternal jailor steals

a drop of light from your oil, my country...)

Oh to lie down on the sprayed roof on a moonlit summer night

and listen like a child to my mother's stories...

if not for those relentless eyes

I would have counted the stars from my roof.

Cala-bala-purtaqala

    My uncle told me bring the...cala,

       Wheee.[49]

...Open a sardine can

    and lie down in it

       to sleep.

"هيلةْ يا رُمَّانةْ

... الحلوةْ زعلانةْ[50]... لماذا عكَّرتَ مزاجي

في عيدِ الميلادِ

بأنغامِ شخيرِكَ، يا سيِّد حرزٍ،...

كأنَّةِ قمحٍ تتكسَّرُ تحتَ حجارِ الطاحونةِ.

أفتحُ رأسي، وأُنظِّفُهُ من

قَشِّ الأحلامِ، لعلِّي...

وبعيداً... تُومضُ أضواءُ السياراتِ، ثريَّاتُ الحفلاتِ، مصابيحُ المدنِ المُكتظَّةِ بالرغباتِ،

تسيلُ ثراءً، عهراً مبذولاً.

وأنا القابعُ في الظلمةِ وحدي

(يا ليلُ، الصبـ...حُ متى غدُهُ...[51]

أرِقَ القنَّاصُ وأرَّقهُ...) ... ليلٌ من قصديرٍ، يهبطُ حتى نافذتي،

تنكسِرُ المرآةُ إلى نصفين،

فأُبصِرُ شيخاً هرماً يُشبِهُني،

يتبعُهُ حشدُ طفولاتٍ فطمتها الحربُ.

ألمُّ شظايا المرآةِ فتجرحُني الكلماتُ.

يسيلُ دمي فوقَ الزئبقِ منساباً حتى رفَّ مُخيِّلتي.

أفتحُ ألبومَ الصحبِ

وأبكي مَنْ ضاعوا في ليلِ الجبهاتِ، المدنِ، الذكرى...

"جئنا باللورياتِ الخشبيَّةِ، مكبوسينَ كتمرٍ في الأخصافِ"[52]

لماذا تشطرُني الحربُ إلى نصفينِ،

لماذا يغدو الليلُ كجزمةِ جنديٍّ أثقلَها الطينُ،

تجوسُ بصدري.

سأجرِّبُ أن أكتبَ في العتمةِ، مُلتصِّاً ضوءَ التنوير

(تناقشنا حتى آخرةِ الليلِ

عن الشِعرِ الثوريِّ وخوفِ النقّادِ.

امتعضَ الحلّاقُ أبو شكرٍ،

Hailah ya rummanah

...*Beauty is sorrowful* [50]...Why did you ruin her mood

at Christmas?

The sound of your snore, Mr Herez,

      is like barley being ground under a millstone.

        I open my head, and clean out

               the chaff of dreams, maybe I shall...

And far away the car lights blink at the posh chandeliers, and the city

lights rage with desire, dripping with wealth and prostitution.

And I'm lying alone in the darkness,

(*O night, when will morning come?* [51]

The sniper had insomnia...) A night of tin falling past my window.

  The mirror broke in two.

   Then I see a senile man just like me

followed by childhoods weaned by war.

I gather the shards of glass and am wounded by the words.

My blood flows on mercury until it touches my imagination.

I open my album of friends

      and weep for those wasted at the front, the cities, the memories.

        Compressed like dates in a basket, we came in trucks. [52]

Why does the war break me in two?

Why does night become a soldier's boot weighed down by mud,

stamping on my chest?

I shall try to write at night, stealing light from flares.

(We talked until morning

    about revolutionary poetry and fear of the critics.

    The barber, Abo Skukur, got fed up.

أخرجَ من طرفِ البطانيّةِ رأساً كثّاً

لا يتقنُ غيرَ الشتمِ.

سلاماً، يا وطنَ الشعراءِ المنسيين

بلا وطنٍ.. لو أملكُ وقتاً لدلفتُ إلى

المكتبةِ الوطنيّةِ

أستعرضُ أسماءَ الكتبِ المبلوعةِ

في كرشِ رقيبِ المطبوعاتِ...

– لماذا قصَّ رقيبُ الشعرِ سمائي الأولى،

– ولماذا أطفأتِ السيجارةَ في غضبٍ بيروقراطيٍّ ومضيتِ

بأولِ تكسيٍّ (رنَّ الهاتفُ،

كان القلبُ على الخطِّ الثاني

يتساءلُ عن امكانيةِ عشقِ امرأةٍ أخرى...

أطبقتُ السماعةَ في أدبٍ جمٍّ

فالتفتت امرأتي للقلقِ المفضوحِ على شفتي) –

مَنْ يسألُ عنّي في هذا القيظِ اللاهبِ،

مرّت أشجارُ الصَّفْصافِ على شبّاكي

فحَلَمْتُ بفيءِ ضفائرها.

كان النهرُ بعيداً والمخفرُ ممتلئاً بالموقوفين،

فنمتُ إلى الصبحِ على الأرضِ المنقوعةِ بالبولِ.

حَلَمتُ بساقيها يلتفّانِ على ظهري،

فتسيلُ على السروِ لزوجتُها.

كانتْ ساقا الشرطيِّ تنامانِ على عنقي والفجرُ قصيّاً.

قلتُ لها قلبي أدفأ من شقّتِهِ

فمضتْ هازئةً تَعْلُكُ ايقاعَ المتداركِ

نحوَ المصعدِ،[53]

قلتُ لها ما أوحشَ باباً لا يَطْرُقُها أحدٌ...

88

He stuck out of the blankets a thick-haired head

that was good for nothing but swearing.

Hello, country of forgotten poets

without a nation) if I had time I would go into

the national library

and list the names of books swallowed

in the belly of the censor.

– *Why has the censor of poetry cut my first sky?*

– *And why did you angrily stub out your cigarette?* She flagged down

the first taxi (the phone rang,

a heart was on the other end

wondering about the possibility of loving another woman.

I hung up the phone with extreme politeness.

My woman turned to me because of the worried look on my face) –

who asks about me in this scorching heat?

Willows passed by my window

and I dreamed about the shadows of her braids.

The river was far away and the police station filled with detainees

and I slept until morning on ground soaked with piss

and dreamed about her legs around my back.

Then her juices flowed onto the cypress.

The policeman was resting his legs on my neck and morning was far off.

I said to her *My heart is warmer than his apartment.*

She walked away towards the elevator chewing the rhythm of

Mutadarik metre.[53]

I told her *Doors that aren't knocked on by anyone are very gloomy.*

89

ضغطتُ زرّاً فانطلقَ المصعدُ

يحملُ أعذبَ إيقاعٍ للمتداركِ

مرَّ بتاريخِ الشِعرِ)

سيشتمُني النقّادُ على هذا الهذيانِ المرِّ.

سيُصفعُ في وجهي بابُ النشرِ،

ويرجمُني الشعراءُ...

دخلتُ إلى البارِ بصحبةِ نفسيَ

نشربُ نخبَ نقيقِ الشعراءِ.

ضحكنا من نَظّامي الأشعارِ الرسميّةِ، لحّاسي

أحذيةِ الجنرالِ، المُمْتَلِيء الرأسِ بروثِ الأبقارِ.

التفتَ النادلُ ممتعضاً للمخبولِ الأشعثِ

يقرأُ – منفعلَ النبرةِ – شِعراً:

جائعةٌ كلُّ نمورِكَ يا جنرالُ

فكيف ستنزلُ منها؟

صفَّقَ بعضُهمُ

وبكى الآخرُ،

لكنّي لم أبكِ.

كنتُ أرى وجةَ الأشعثِ

– في مرآةِ البارِ –

يراقصُ حزني،

فدنوتُ من المخبولِ،

تقاسمنا العرقَ المرَّ،

الزمنَ المرَّ.

تصافحنا

– موعدُنا السبتُ...

90

She pressed a button and the elevator

moved to the rhythm of Mutadarik.

        It was the most beautiful poem in the history of poetry –

        I shall be cursed by the critics for this bitter babbling.

     The doors of publishers will slap my face,

           I'll be stoned by poets.

I took myself into a bar

       and drank a toast to croaking poets.

    We laughed at the official poetry writers, the wipers

   of the General's shoes, whose heads are filled with cow muck.

The waiter turned his head to the crazy man with shaggy hair

       saying – in an agitated tone –

         All your tigers are hungry General,

so how you are going to escape from them?

Some of them clapped.

Others wept

But I didn't weep,

I could see Al-Ashath's face

      in the bar's mirror

      dancing with my grief.

I approached the crazy man

      and we shared the bitter wine,

         the bitter time.

           We shook hands.

– *Our appointment is on Saturday.*

‒ مساءً؟...

‒ لا تنسَ...

‒ في نفسِ البارِ...

مساءَ السبتِ، رأيتُ الأشعثَ يدلفُ للبارِ، بدلٍ بيروقراطيٍّ،

مصفوفَ الشَّعرِ، بصحبةِ سيِّدةٍ...

ها هو يدنو من طاولتي، مرتدياً ربطةَ عنقٍ فاخرةٍ.

قمتُ أصافحُهُ.

فتجاهلَني دونَ مبالاةٍ، مجتازاً كفِّي الممدودةَ...

يتبعهُ النادلُ منحنياً حتى الطاولةِ المحجوزةِ في الركنِ...

تداريتُ الخجلَ القرويَّ أمامَ الرُّوّادِ،

وأمعنتُ بشربِ الخمرةِ حتى...

‒ حتى أنتَ؟!...

قُبيلَ الفجرِ أفقتُ على نفسي مرميّاً

فوقَ رصيفِ الشارعِ

أهذي...

‒ كيف تغيَّرتِ الدنيا يا عَبُّودُ؟

ستكنسُكَ الريحُ

رماداً مخلوطاً

من كتبٍ ومنيٍّ وخساراتٍ.

فتزوَّدْ ‒ قبلَ سقوطِ أمانيكَ الفِجَّةِ ‒

من شمِّ عرارِ النسوةِ،

فالمدنُ الإسمنتيّةُ لا تبكي جثَّتَكَ الملقاةَ

أمامَ عمودِ الهاتفِ

حين تموتُ من السُكرِ أو الحبِّ... (أسابقُ موتي

– Night…?

– Don't forget.

– In the same bar.

Saturday night, I saw the crazy man come in, dressed like a bureaucrat,

groomed hair, and with a lady.

    Here he was, getting closer to my table, wearing a fancy tie.

  I stood up to shake his hand

    and he ignored me, disregarding my extended paw,

      followed by a bent-backed waiter to the reserved table in the corner.

I hid my embarrassment in front of the patrons,

        I plunged into the wine until…

– Even you?!…

Before dawn, I woke up, chucked out

      on the street,

            in a hung-over state.

– How did the world change Aboud?

The wind will sweep you away,

    a mixed ash

        of books, semen and losses.

Then – have you enough supplies before your ripe dreams fall –

make the most of the scent of women.

    The concrete cities don't weep over your laid-out corpse.

        In front of the telephone pole

            as you die of drunkenness or love, I race against death

في عينِ القنّاصِ.

العصرُ سباقٌ محمومٌ. أفتحُ عيني وسطَ رمادِ الأشياءِ،

أرى وطني يعلو

فوقَ هتافِ المحتشدينَ، رصاصاً محموماً)

الغربةُ تعصرُ عمري كلماتٍ.

مَنْ يشري كلماتِ الغرباءِ بشبرٍ

من وطنٍ،

مَنْ يشربُ نخبَ الغرباءِ إذا فاضتْ أقداحُ الروحِ

على طاولةٍ في ركنِ البارِ.

صرختُ حزيناً: يا وطني

فارتجَّتْ جدرانُ الزنزانةِ: يـ......اا!!...

... واقتسمَ الحرّاسُ بقايا الأحرفِ

والتبغِ المخبوءِ ببطانيّةِ

إحدى المسجوناتِ

قُبيلَ الإعدامِ...

صرختُ أحبّكَ يا دمعَ النجماتِ على سفحِ الجبلِ

المحروثِ بدوشكاتِ الجندِ،

أحبّكَ يا بوحَ البرعمِ تحتَ قميصِ التلميذةِ،

يا أشعاري الممنوعةَ، يا أضلاعي الموقودةَ

فوقَ الجسرِ مصابيحاً، يا ميمَ الحلوةِ،

يا ألقي وجنوني وبكائي،

يا نهرَ طفولتِنا المُتَعرِّجَ

بين بساتينِ التِّكِّي

والمركزِ، يا خجلَ الفتياتِ

من النظراتِ

الأولى...

94

under the sniper's eye.

Time is a frantic race, I open my eyes among the ashes of things.

I see my country rising

over the cheers of the crowd like frenzied bullets.

Alienation is squeezing my life into words.

Who buys the stranger's words in exchange for a handspan

of my country?

Who drinks the stranger's toast if the soul's glass has overflowed

onto a table in the corner of the bar?

I shouted sadly: *O my country*

so the walls of the cell shook: Oh!!

And the guards shared the scraps of letters

and hidden tobacco in the blanket of

one of the prisoners

before she was executed.

I shouted *I love you, tears of stars on the tips of mountains*

ploughed by the machine guns of soldiers,

I love you, O girl blossoming under your student's blouse.

O my forbidden poems. O my ribs burning

across the bridge like lanterns. O pretty M.

O my spark, my madness, my crying.

O river of our youth winding

between the mulberry orchards

and the secret police station.

O shyness of young girls'

first glances.

95

. . . .

. . . .

. . . .

خذْ أوردتي لو نضبَ الزيتُ،

أنا اخشى الظلمةَ،

أخشى الجدرانَ الضيِّقةَ السوداءَ تحاصرُ عمري البَضَّ.

أتَذْكُرُ؟ كمْ ضيَّفنا السَجّانُ فنمتُ

على فخِذِك والأرضِ المرشوشةِ بالبولِ إلى الفجرِ.

أتَذْكُرُ؟ كمْ كنّا نَحْلُمُ بالشمسِ وراءَ

القضبانِ، تُفَلِّي شَعرَ ليالينا الكثَّ من القملِ ورائحةِ الفَسْوِ.

أتَذْكُرُ؟ ها هي شمسُ اللهِ تُطِلُّ

على ساحاتِك كلَّ صباحٍ.

ها

هي

أسرابُ التلميذاتِ يُواصِلنَ الغنجَ العصريَّ أمامَك، بذلاتُ

العمالِ الماضين إلى الشغلِ، مصابيحُ الشارعِ لمْ تُطفأ

بعدُ، أغاني الگبنجي[54] من المذياعِ، حمائمُ نصبِ

الحُرِّيةِ، زقزقةُ الأشجارِ الممتدَّةِ طولَ الكورنيشِ...

ولكنَّ القنّاصَ القابعَ تحتَ جفوني لا يتركُني أحْلُمُ...

ذي ماسورتُهُ الضيِّقةُ الملساءُ

تحاصرُ عنقي البَضَّ... (لماذا لا تتركُني فوَّهةُ القنّاصِ

أواصِلُ أحلامي

في هذا الفجرِ المتشرِّبِ باليوكالبتوز...؟)

. . . .

. . . .

. . . .

....

....

....

Take my veins if the oil dries up,

I'm afraid of the dark,

I'm afraid of tight black walls surrounding my youth.

Do you remember? How the jailor was our host and I slept

on your thigh on ground sprayed with piss until dawn.

Do you remember? How we used to dream of the sun beyond the

bars, picking lice from the hair of our thick nights and the smell of farts.

Do you remember? This is the sun of God looking down

on your squares every morning.

This

is it:

swarms of girls continue their silly flirting in front of you, men

in work clothes going to work, the streetlights have not been switched

off yet, songs of Al-Gubunchi[54] on the radio, pigeons on the 'Freedom

Monument', the swaying of trees spread out along the boulevard...

But the sniper hiding under my eyelashes does not let me dream...

this smooth, narrow rifle of his

besieges my supple neck (why doesn't the tip of the rifle leave me

to continue my dreams

in this eucalyptus-soaked dawn...?)

....

....

....

ابتدأ القصفُ شديداً هذي الليلة،

فاهتزَّتْ علبُ السردين بنا،

لسنا أحياءً أو أمواتاً:

و [... وُلدتُ، وتوفيتُ،...،

و(لا خللٌ، في القوةِ والقِدْرِ)...]...

تُطوِّقُنا نشراتُ الأخبارِ على الموجاتِ الأخرى،

تتصادمُ فوقَ صخورِ الملجأ، حاملةً زبداً وعواصمَ

بالمني جوب، حروباً، قتلى بالجملةِ، ثوّاراً منفيين، اعلاناً عن

مسحوقِ الحبِّ العذري بالشكولاتا. وغداً من يدري

أين سنُدفنُ؟...، مَنْ لا يملكُ شبراً أو وطناً قد

لا يملكُ قبراً أو كَفناً (تدفنُنا جرّافاتُ الأمريكان، بعيداً

في الصحراءِ، فتخرجُنا حيواناتُ البرِّ، فيدفنُنا الأهلُ،

فتخرجُنا جرّافاتُ الحرسِ الجمهوريِّ،

فيدفنُنا الـ....)

....

....

....

كانَ المُؤرِّخُ يُدخِلُ مِنْ ثقْبِ إبرتِه

جَمَلاً أعرجاً

كلّما صاحَ فيه الخليفةُ:

أين وصلتَ بتدوينِ سيرتِنا

قالَ ما قالهُ المتنبي

سوى الرومِ خلفَكَ رومٌ

وما خلفَ تاريخِنا حرجٌ

فأن نسيَ المستعينُ ببغدادَ

The bombardment began heavily tonight,

    shaking us like sardines in a can.

        We are not dead or alive:

And (...*I was born, and died...*)

And (...*no mules or soldiers killed, no losses or gains...*)

News bulletins make us switch to other frequencies

which crisscross the stony trench carrying scum and capital cities

in miniskirts, wars, mass murder, exiled revolutionaries, an advert for a

platonic, chocolate-flavoured aphrodisiac. And tomorrow, who knows

where we will be buried? We who have no hand-span of land and can

own no grave or shroud. (The American bulldozers bury us, far away in

the desert, then the wild animals dig us up, so our families bury us again,

then the bulldozers of the Republican Guard dig us up,

then we are buried by the...)

....

....

....

    The historian would have the eye of his needle

        with a limping camel slipped in.

        At every roar, the Caliph would shout at him:

When did you come into my life-history?

He would say, as Al-Mutanabi has said,

There are also Romans behind you; so where do you turn?

    Behind our history there is embarrassment.

If Al-Musta'in in Baghdad forgot

دَفْعَ رواتبِ حرّاسِهِ

أكلوهُ

وخرُّوهُ

في الطرقاتِ

ومستنصرٍ باسمِهِ أم عليه

سيحكمُ في الأرضِ ستين عاماً [إلهي،

أُبتلينا

بهذي الملوكِ، التي

لا تقومُ من العرشِ

إلّا لتقضيَ حاجاتِها] سَيُزوِّج ابنتَهُ

من عصا طغرل بك تدبُّ

بسبعين عاماً

إلى قبرِهِ،

صفقةً تتوزَّعُ بين:

الخلافةِ

والباهِ...

والكاعبُ الغرُّ تجهلُ دورَ النساءِ

بصنعِ الحكوماتِ

– يا سيّدي، كلّما احتبستْ

في مثانةِ روميّةٍ، درةٌ

حبستْ حاكماً

والجنرالُ بعزلتِهِ...

كلّما شقَّ صوتُ المؤذّنِ، جُبَّةَ هذا الفضاءِ

المكلَّلِ فوقَ جفونِ العبادِ، سيلبسُ عِمَّتَهُ

ويَؤُمُّ الجموعَ التي تستظلُّ مُكَبِّرةً باسمِهِ

وهو لاهٍ بتعديلِ تكَّةِ سروالِهِ.

to give his troops their wages

they would have eaten him up

and shitted him out

on the roads.

Al–Mustansir, great by name but not in reality,

presided on earth for sixty years (O Lord

      we were woefully afflicted

         with those kings, from

             whose thrones they never rose

          except to go to the toilet) will be marrying his daughter

          to Taghril Beg's crutch which has been lurching

        for seventy years

      towards its grave.

It's a deal between

    Caliphate,

    copulation

and a shapely young girl who doesn't yet know about the role of women

in founding governments.

– *O sir, when will there be a pearl*

      in some Roman girl's vagina

         that she saves for the Governor.

The General in his privacy…

(every so often, the voice of the muezzin splits this *jubbah* of space

that crowns the eyelids of God's servants…) will put on his turban,

      and address the congregation who are shouting his name

         whilst he is busy adjusting his underwear.

فاذا أغلقوا جفنَ حبَّابةٍ أغلقَ الجامعَ الأمويَّ،
وظلَّ يلوبُ وراءَ العمودِ
وينحلُّ،
ينحلُ.. حتى تناهى
إلى قبرِها،
مثلَ رجعِ صدىً حائرٍ،
بين عرشِ الغرامِ
وعرشِ الخلافةِ
والمسلمونَ على بابِهِ
يلطمونَ ضياعَ الحصونِ
فتحتجُّ سيِّدةُ القصرِ:
ــ ما هكذا، يا مُؤرِّخُ،
تُروى
حكايا
الملوك

....
....
....

والجنرالُ بعزلتِهِ
ناشقاً في الفخاخِ عبيرَ الوعولِ:
(ألذُّ من المسكِ هذي الروائحُ.
كانتْ تهبُّ على قصرِهِ
من بساتين بغدادَ،
حاملةً جثثَ الخارجينَ
مسلوخةً والرماحُ تشكُّ فضاءَ التباريحِ في دمِهِ المسكِ،

102

Should the eyelid of Habbaba close, the Umayyad Mosque will shut.

He moves behind the column

dwindles and dwindles

   until he fades from sight

          into her grave,

just as an echo drifts bewildered

            between the throne of adoration

            and the throne of the Caliphate.

When Moslems come to his door

   slapping their heads over their loss of lands

the lady of the palace will thus protest:

   – Nay, O historian, that's no way to talk

        about kings,

          their stories

           should inform.

…………………………

…………………………

…………………………

The General in his solitude

breathes in, trapped in a goaty smell

(more delightful than musk are the scents

         blowing into his palace

from the orchards of Baghdad,

     from inside the skinned corpses of transgressors)

       while the spears make a space of torments in his musky blood.

يتركُ دولتَهُ

بيدِ الخيزرانِ،[55]

تُقيمُ الولاةَ وتعزلُهم،

فيرى قهرمانتَها[56]

تَتَرَبَّعُ في مجلسِ البرلمانِ،

تَرُدُّ المظالمَ...

– سيِّدتي، سرقوا عنزتي...

– ما فُقدتْ عنزةٌ في سوادِ العراقِ،

ففي عنقي دَينُها...

– ... ثمَّ ناموا مَعَ امرأتي، وابنتي

– إذا كانَ مِنْ قُبُلٍ،

فبراءٌ جنودُ الخليفةِ

لا يطأونَ النساءَ الحصيناتِ

إلّا مِن الدبرِ،

ولتسألنَّ – إذا راودتكَ الشكوكُ –

مُؤخَّرتي...

تقرعُ لاهيةً جرسَ خلخالِها،

من قيانٍ وليلو...

فيُطلُّ من البابِ حارسُها الضخْمُ منتعظاً:

– أمرُ سيِّدتي

فَصِّلوا جُثَّةَ البرمكيِّ

– على بابِ قصرِ الرشيدِ –

ثلاثاً

....

....

....

He left his State

      in the hands of Al-Khaizaran,[55]

who immediately appoints and ousts leaders

and instructs her maid[56]

to sit in Parliament

      and act like a judge…

– *My lady, my goat has been stolen…*

– *No goats have ever been lost in the fields of Iraq,*

      but, upon my honour, I promise to recompense you…

– *Then they slept with my wife and daughter…*

– *If the front of the shirt is torn,*

for sure, the Caliph's soldiers are innocent,

      because they only fuck women

      from behind.

      If in doubt, you can question

           my buttocks…

In amused indulgence, she tinkles the bell of her anklet

      for her chambermaids and pearls.

Then her erect guard emerges from the doorway:

– *Yes, my Lady,*

the corpse of Al-Barmaki has been cut in three

      at the gate of the

           Al-Rasheed palace.

. . . .

. . . .

. . . .

ومن شُرفةِ المجدِ،

يبكي الرشيدُ لياليهِ

لا نجمةٌ غيرُ هذي الدموعِ،

مُزَقْزَقَةٍ،

فوقَ خدِّ السماءِ

تُظلّلُها غيمةٌ عبرتْ:

أينما تمطرين، يأتي إليَّ خراجُكِ

لكنَّ هذا الكرى كيف يأتي..

فيسمعُ قهقهةَ الخادماتِ،

بحضنِ النواسيِّ:

لي نحوَ ثغرِكِ هذا الحنينُ يتعتعُني

فأميلُ إلى حانةٍ في الرُّصافةِ

ما لي وللناسٍ يلحوني سَفَهاً[57]

كلّما طفحَ الكأسُ بالذكرياتِ، تذكّرتُ ثغرَ جنانٍ

فماذا يريدُ الخليفةُ منّي

له ملكُهُ...

وليَ الكأسُ مملكةٌ،

لا يحدُّ حباحبَها الجندُ

....

....

....

هذا متاعُكَ؟

أين ستحملُهُ

أيّها العابرُ المستحيلَ

بنعلين من ورقٍ

From the balcony of glory,

     Al-Rasheed sobs away his nights,

no star looms apart from these tears

       rippling

        over the cheek of the sky,

          shadowed by a passing cloud.

Wherever it rains, I reap the crops

so how come I can't sleep?

He hears a maidservant giggle,

     on the lap of Al-Nawsi.

This yearning for your lips makes me drunk

so I lean against a bar in Al-Rusafa.

Why do foolish people blame me?[57]

Like a cup brimming with memories, Jinan's lips will restore me.

What more does the Caliph want from me?

He has dominion over everything…

but to me, this cup is my whole kingdom

     and its bubbles have no limits.

………………………………

………………………………

………………………………

These things belong to you,

where should you take them?

O you, impossible passer-by

     with only a pair of paper slippers,

راحلاً عن دروبٍ سترثيك
كلُّ الدروبِ مهادٌ
تُبدِّلُها بمهادٍ
ولكنَّ نفسَك كيف تُبدِّلُها؟

....

....

....

انفجرتْ قنبلةٌ وتشظَّتْ موتاً أسودَ.. ما زالتْ حِصَّتُنا
بعدُ.. تعثَّر محمودٌ بصوتِ المذياعِ المغناجِ
فأطفأهُ في ركلةٍ بسطالٍ، فتنائر أمعاءً خائسةً
وحبالَ غسيلٍ لأكاذيبِ الحكَّامِ. نظرتُ إلى سقفِ
الجينكو المهتزِّ تمنَّيتُ بأن أُخرِجَ رأسي لأرى
الصحوَ الممتدَّ... (عيونَ الموتى الشاخصةَ النظراتِ إلى اللهِ)
تمنَّيتُ بأن أُخرِجَ قلبي من معطفِهِ الخاكي وأريهِ
بلادي (ما صنعتْ أسنانُ السرفاتِ بها)
لِمَ لم تخلقْ للموتِ عيوناً، يا ربِّي، قد يعطفُ حينَ
يرانا – بالأحلامِ البيضاء المكويَّة والأعمارِ الغضَّةِ، لا نملكُ حولاً
أو قولاً في كلِّ حروبِ التاريخِ الممتدَّةِ من عصرِ المُدْيَةِ حتى
الليزرِ – محضَ جنودٍ يلعبُ فينا ملكانِ غبيَّانِ على
رقعةِ شطرنجِ الأوطانِ... تمنَّيتُ بأن أعبرَ هذا النهرَ المتدفِّق
نحو... فماءتْ في الركنِ القطَّةُ.. مَنْ جاءَ بكِ الساعة
ترتجفين أمام أزيزِ الطلقاتِ وتلتصقين بجسمي
هلْ أبعدُها؟
فالقنَّاصُ الأجلفُ لا يترصِّدُ رأسَكِ بل رأسي
لكنْ من يدري قد تُخْطِيءُ هذي الفوَّهةُ العمياءُ

wandering from the pathways that cry for you.

All paths are stretches

   replaced by other stretches

but for you, how can you change yourself?

  ....

  ....

  ....

A bomb exploded and shattered into black death...but our share is still
waiting for us...Mahmoud stumbled over the sound of the flirty radio,
switched it off with a kick that spilled out its rotting intestines
and washing lines of governors' lies. I looked at the juddering,
corrugated-iron ceiling. I wanted to stick my head out to see the
stretching wakefulness...(the eyes of the dying always gaze at God)...
I wanted to pull my heart out from its soldier's uniform and show Him
my country (and what the teeth of the tanks have done to it).
O God, why didn't you make the eyes of Death more kind when he sees
us with our smooth, white dreams and tender years, having no power
and no say in the history of all wars from the time of blades to the time
of bombs – just soldiers; two stupid kings are playing with us on the
nation's chess board. I wanted to cross this overflowing river
towards...the cat meowed in the corner...*How did you get here,*
trembling in front of the sputtering gunshots and clinging to me...
shall I shift her out the way?
The thuggish sniper doesn't want your head, but mine,
but who knows, his blind muzzle might make a mistake.

فلا أحدٌ يضمن عمرَكِ أو عمري..

مَنْ يضمنُ – في هذا العالمِ – عمراً يتقاطعُ

في عينيْ قنّاصٍ...

في عِزِّ الصيفِ، ركضتُ وراءَ القطةِ، منسلّاً من بابِ البيتِ.

انتبهتْ أمي، لكنّي...) قلتُ أُخَبّئُ عمري بين الأحراشِ

المتمايلةِ السيقانِ مع الريحِ، وأعبرُ هذا الموجَ – الفرح المترقرقَ،

مختنقاً بالغصّاتِ (سلاماً يا شطَّ الكوفةِ،

يا نزقَ الصبيةِ يا ما خبّأتُ الدشداشةَ، بين غصونِ

الصَّفْصَافِ، ويا ما سرقوها، فلبستُ سياطَ

أبي، ورجعتُ إلى البيتِ. فماذا ألبسُ لو سرقَ القنّاصُ

ثيابَ العمرِ) وثانيةً عدتُ إلى النهرِ، وثالثةً

للعينين السوداوين، وعاشرةً بالركلاتِ إلى السجنِ، وألفاً

لصفيرِ الليلِ. تلمّستُ طريقي في العتمةِ كان القنّاصُ

يُثقّبُ بالناظورِ عباءةَ ليلِ الإبريسِمِ، يلظمُها

بخيوطِ الطلقاتِ. اللعنة ماذا لو أرى

القطّةَ قدّامَ الموضعِ، منتظراً ماذا يحدثُ. نحنُ تساوينا

بأواني الحربِ المستطرقةِ. انتفضتْ روحي ولعنتُ حماقةَ أفكارِ

الحربِ. تخيّلتُ الجسدَ الناعمَ منخوباً يتلوّى بين الرملِ

وكفّي الممدودةِ بركةً دمٍ. لذتُ بزاويتي

أتحاشى طولَ الليلِ مواءَ العينين اللامعتين، دنوتُ

أهدهدُ رأسَ المسكينةِ معتذراً، فأختبأتْ خلفَ الجلكانِ

(دنوتُ فأزَّ الباصُ سريعاً، وأندفعتْ امرأةٌ ريّا نحوي في العقدِ الرابعِ

(– في عينيه أبعدُ من امرأةٍ..

(لا بأسَ اخترنا مصطبةً نائيةً قربَ الجرفِ المُعشبِ. (كانتْ

تتحدّثُ عن أحلامِ طفولتِها العرجاءِ وأطباقِ الوحدةِ

والزوجِ المشلولِ بمعركةِ الخفجي (يشردُ قلبُ الشاعرِ

No one guarantees your life or mine.

Who guarantees – in this world – a life caught in the cross-hairs

of a sniper…

In the hot summer, I ran out of the house, after a cat,

my mother noticed, but… I said *I can hide my life among the jungle*

of boughs swayed by the wind, then cross the waves – the glittering joy,

suffocated by torments. (Peace be upon you, riverbank of Al-Kufa,

and the rashness of the youth who hid his *dishdasha* among the branches

of the weeping willow, where it got stolen, and he put on a dress of his

father's lashes when he got home. So what can I wear if the sniper steals

the clothes of life?) Secondly, I came back to the river, thirdly for her

black eyes, tenthly with kicks into the prison, thousandthly to the

whistling night. I groped my way in darkness where the sniper was

poking holes in night's cloak with his field glasses, sewing it up with a

thread of bullets. Damn! What would happen if I threw

the cat in front of the trench. We are both the same in the

communicating vessels of war. My soul erupted and cursed the folly of

war. I imagined the soft, perforated fur twisting between the sand

and my outstretched palm in a pool of blood. I repaired to my corner

to avoid a long night of meowing and shiny eyes. Apologising, I came

closer, stroking the head of the poor cat hidden behind the jerrycans.

(I came closer and the bus jerked forwards. A fat woman of forty,

rushed towards me, filled with desire;) in his eyes are far-away women…

(It didn't matter, we selected a far-away bank near a grassy cliff, she was

talking about her crippled childhood dreams, the dishes of loneliness,

and the husband paralysed at the battle of Khafgy), the heart of the poet

111

تحتَ قناطرِ جفنيكِ مهيباً كالبحرِ...[58] (تأمّلتُ
الزرَّ المفتوحَ، ارتبكتْ بعضَ الشيءِ،
وغطّتْ بيديها شبقَ
النهرِ المتدفّق (... مسّدتُ الوبرَ الناعمَ في رأسِ القطّةِ،
فارتجفتْ تَرمُقُني بمواءٍ مرِّ
(– هلْ عِنْدَكَ كبريت؟
– لا...
كانتْ نافذةُ الليلِ مُرصّعةً بنجومِ الرغباتِ
احترقتْ أعشابُ النهرِ ولمْ يبقَ على المصطبةِ الخشبيّةِ
غيرُ بقايا الكرزاتِ ونصفِ الزرِّ المقطوعِ)
انتظرتُ باصاً آخر
ما زالَ الليلُ لذيذاً كالكرزاتِ
قطعنا الشارعَ مشياً تحتَ رَذاذِ نوافيرِ البوحِ الليليِّ
(سأعْطِيكِ إذاً عنواني...) انفتَحتْ بابٌ في منعطفِ الدربونةِ: كانت
أصغرَ بالشَعرِ المبلولِ تناثرَ يخفي نصفَ ملامحِها (– هل عِنْدَكِ كبريت؟
– لا) قادتني في عتمةِ دهليزٍ،
أتَلَمّسُ ردفيها وطريقي المتعثّرَ...
رغمَ العتمةِ أبصرتُ فحيحَ الرغبةِ في عينيها السوداوين ونصفَ الزرِّ المقطوعِ...
(– البارحةَ انقطعَ التيارُ) دنوتُ من الأزرارِ الأخرى.
اندلقَ النهدُ شهيّاً من شقِّ الثوبِ.
انفرجتْ شفتاها،
فانتصبَ الجذعُ المحنيُّ على النهرِ (ارفعْني في قاربِكَ الناحلِ،
خصراً يتكسّرُ في الريحِ،
وشَعراً مجنوناً يصهلُ فوق براري صدرِكَ
سَدّدْهُ إليَّ، قويّاً، محتقناً،
وافتضَّ حنيني.
فأنا الفارعةُ المنذورةُ منذُ طفولةِ نهدي للشبقِ الطافحِ

112

strayed under the bridges of your eyelids like a great sea...[58] (I stared at
her opened shirt button, she was confused,

> she covered with her own hands the salaciousness of the
> overflowing river)...I stroked the soft fur on the cat's head
> as it trembled and gazed at me with sour mew.
> (– *Do you have a light?* –
> – *No...*).

The window of night was inlaid with stars of desire.
The grass on the river bank was burnt, on the wooden table
there was nothing but cherry stones and half a button).
She waited for another bus.
Night still tasted of cherries.

> We walked across the street under a drizzle of intimate whispers
(*so, I'll give you my address...*) A door opened in the narrow street: she
was younger with wet hair hiding half her face (– *Have you got a light?*
– *No*). She led me into a dark passage,
I was feeling her buttocks in my stumbling way.
Despite darkness, I saw lust hissing in her black eyes and half a
button...(yesterday the electricity was off) I undid the other buttons.
Her delicate breast emerged from the split in her dress.
Her lips opened widely, tenderly.
The curved trunk rose above the river (hold me up in your small boat,
waist swaying in the wind
and crazy hair neighing on the deserts of your chest.
Push it towards me strongly, full of life and vitality,
and satisfy my desire.
I am tall and since maturity I vowed that my breasts would light up

في عينيكَ، ادفعُهُ كثيراً،

أكثرَ مِمَّا يحتملُ القلبُ وقاربُكَ الغائرُ في أحراشي...)

أفرغتُ بقايا القنينةَ في جوفي، ظماً. ثرثرنا حتى

بانَ الخيطُ الأبيضُ في ليلِ الخصلاتِ

المنثورةِ فوق أريكتِها ونُعاسي. اقتربتُ من

مرآةِ الزينةِ (– هل ستجيءُ غداً؟) – لا أدري؟ هل يسمحُ لي

القنّاصُ بيومٍ آخر. مللتُ برأسي بين الصخرِ

قليلاً، وتمدَّدتُ على أكياسِ الرملِ، أُعلّقُ معطف ظَرْفي في

مشجبِ هذا الكونِ المترامي الأحلامِ...

أرى فوقَ خدودِ الليلِ دموعاً متحجّرةً، صعدتْ

من أحداقِ البشرِ الفانين

وظلَّتْ كالنجماتِ

مُعلَّقةً

في أهدابِ اللهِ...

اندلقَ الصبحُ ندياً فوق الزهرِ البريِّ، خرجتُ من الموضعِ

أبحثُ عن أزهارٍ لصباحِكِ

(قلبي قطعٌ متناثرةٌ مَنْ يجمعُها)[59]

مالَ الغُصنُ

على الغُصنِ

وأزَّتْ قربي الطلقةُ

خبَّأت النبضَ المتسارعَ،

بين النسغين الملتصقَين

وقرفصتُ وراءَ الصخرةِ

لا أحملُ غيرَ فُتاتِ الوردِ المتناثرِ

فكَّرتُ بسُخريَّةٍ: هلْ يُقتلُ إنسانٌ يحملُ زهراً

ماذا يمكنُ أنْ يجني هذا الأحمقُ من موتي . هلْ يبني بيتاً

بنوافذَ واسعةٍ من جمجمتي... أيُحبُّ الشِعرَ؟

114

your eyes with desire; push it more and more,

more than the heart can endure your boat entering my jungles...)

I emptied the rest of the bottle into my stomach, thirst. We chatted until

a thread of light appeared on her sofa and on the blackness of her tousled

curls, strewn over the sofa and my sleepiness. She tidied her hair at her

dressing table (– *Will you come tomorrow? – I don't know.*) Will the

sniper grant me another day? l leaned my head among the rocks for a

while and rested on the sandbags, hanging my coat on the peg of the

wide, dreamy universe...

I see on the cheeks of night fossilised tears rise up

from the eyes of decayed human beings

and stay like stars

       hung

          on the lashes of God...

Dawn appeared wet on the wildflowers, I left the trench

looking for flowers for your morning

(my heart is scattered into pieces, who collects them?).[59]

      One branch bent down

           to another

and a bullet whizzed near me.

I hid my racing pulse

     between the two sticky saps

         and squatted behind a rock

with the remnants of scattered flowers.

I thought ironically: *can a man be killed who is carrying flowers?*

What can this fool gain from my death. Will he build a house

with big windows from my skull...does he like poetry?

أجرَّبتُ كتابةَ شِعرٍ لفتاتِكَ؟ ما طولُ ضفائرِها؟

هل مسكتْ كفُّكَ شيئاً آخر: فرشةَ ألوانٍ، طفلاً،

خصرَ امرأةٍ، زهرةَ غاردينيا؟...

أبصرتُ القنّاصَ وراءِ الصخرةِ يرقبُ أحلامي عن كثبٍ

لا بأسَ ألمْ تتورَّمْ عيناكَ من الرصدِ لعنقي؟

مَنْ يدري قد يسخرُ منّي الآن لأنّي.. (أطبقتُ البابَ

ففرَّ الشوقُ الغافي في عينيها الواسعتين، وفرَّ ابني من لعبتِهِ

وتشبَّثَ في عنقي) هذا العنقِ المطلوبِ تحسَّستُ

دبيبَ النبضِ به، في غرفِ التعذيبِ السوداءِ، فأدركتُ بأنّي ما زلتُ..

[– أريد قطاراً، يا بابا... لا تنسَ

أصغيتُ لأنفاسِ القنّاصِ – بهذي الساعةِ –

هادئةً كالفجرِ الأجوفِ...

سَدَّدتُ الفوَّهةَ السوداءَ إلى عينيهِ، وأصغيتُ لأنفاسي

لاهثةً يقطعُها صوتُ حفيفِ شرائطِ طفلتِهِ البيضِ (– ألمْ

يأتِ بابا؟) اختلجتْ في عينيِّ سنينُ اليتمِ،

وذابتْ في شفتيِّ زوجتِهِ أجوبةٌ شتَّى...) انطبقتْ بابُ البيتِ.

الإصبعُ فوق زنادِ الـ.... لو أضغطُهُ.

التمعتْ في هلعٍ مجنونٍ عيناها الواسعتان. اقتربتْ نحوي

(هل يأتي بابا؟)... لا أدري، وانهمرَ اللبلابُ

على صدري المخنوقِ، ثقيلاً مرًّا. قمتُ لأغسلَ وجهي

ثانيةً... فكَّرتُ بماذا كان يُفكِّرُ في هذي اللحظةِ؟

هذا المتأرجحُ في حبلٍ مشدودٍ بين الموتِ وعنقي المهزولِ.

رأيتُ شرائطَها، مرجَ طفولاتٍ وزنابقَ تخفقُ في

الريحِ أمامي، وتطولُ، تطولُ – متى يأتي

بابا؟ يقطعُها صوتُ قطارٍ ينحبُ... هل يأتي بابا؟

لا أدري، لا أدري، كلٌّ يحمِلُ موتَ الآخر في

كفّيهِ... أتسمعُني يا هذا القنّاصُ الأبلهُ: كلٌّ يحمِلُ بينَ

116

Do you try writing poetry to your girlfriend? How long are her plaits?

Did your hand hold something else: a brush for painting,

the waist of a woman, a gardenia?...

I saw the sniper watching my dreams nearby.

It doesn't matter, aren't your eyes swollen from watching my neck?

Who knows he may laugh at me now because...(*Shut the door,*

the sleepy yearning in her wide eyes; my son threw down his toy

and clung to my neck) this desirable neck that I felt the

crawling pulse inside, in the black torture room, I realised that I'm still...

[– *I want a train, Dad...don't forget...*]

I listened to the sniper's breathing – very quiet –

quiet as the hollow dawn...

I aimed the black muzzle at his eyes, I listened carefully to my hurried

breath, breaking across it, the swish of his daughter's white ribbon (– *has*

my Daddy come yet?...the years of orphan-hood rose before my eyes

and his wife's answers melted on her lips...). The door of the house was

shut. The finger is on the trigger...if I press it...

Crazy terror shone in her wide eyes. She came towards me

(*when will my Daddy come?*)...I don't know, the bindweed flew heavily

against my choked chest, dense and sour. I got up to wash my face

again...I wondered what he was thinking at that moment?

The sniper was swinging on the rope between death and my weak neck.

I saw her ribbon like a meadow of childhood and lilies fluttering in the

wind in front of me, it got longer and longer – *when will my Daddy*

come? interrupted by the wailing of a train...*when will Dad come?*

I don't know, I don't know, each is carrying the death of the other in his

palms...do you hear me you doltish sniper: each carries between his

117

أصابعِهِ المشدودةِ فوق زنادِ الرشاشةِ، أرملةً ويتيماً...
مسَّحتُ دموعي في خجلٍ من نفسي...]
يا ربِّي، ما أتفههُ عمر الإنسانِ بهذا الشرقِ الداعرِ.
مِنْ بابِ المسلخِ حتى بابِ المخفرِ
(لا تتكاسلْ كالعادةِ، دورُكَ حان، بملءِ الجلكان...)"

....

....

....

وأذكرُ...
[خلفَ انكسارِ المساءاتِ
خلفَ العباءاتِ
ضجّتْ محلتُنا بالعويلِ على بابِهم
– قِيلَ جاؤوا بتابوتِهِ
لُفَّ بالعلمِ الوطنيِّ

– عَبُّودُ؟

– لا

– أخوهُ؟

– ...

– وعَبُّودُ أين؟

– ...

...

عَبُّودُ في السجنِ يركلُهُ الحارسُ الفظُّ
يُشعِلُ سيجارةً ثّمَّ يُطفئُها
فوق طبلةِ خصيتِهِ
... فتَنُشُّم المدينةُ رائحةَ الشويِّ

gripping fingers and the gun trigger, a widow and an orphan.

...I wiped away my tears ashamed of myself...

God, how trifling the age of Man is in the dissolute East.

From the slaughterhouse to the prison

(*Don't be a lazy sod, it's your turn to fill the jerrycan*).

....

....

....

And I remember,

behind the broken evenings,

behind the cloaks,

the whole village started wailing in front of our neighbour's door.

– They said he was brought home in a coffin

> wrapped in the national flag.

– *Aboud?*

– *No.*

– *His brother?*

– ...

– *And where is Aboud?*

– ...

...

Aboud is in prison, getting kicked by the vicious guard.

The guard lights a cigarette, and stubs it

> out on his balls.

> ...The city smells the barbeque

119

تغفو على جوعِها جرساً يابساً...

من طحينِ القنابلِ،

نصنعُ خبزَ الحياةِ الشهيَّ،

ونحلبُ هذا السرابَ...

جروحي مسيّجةٌ بالكريستالِ،

تضوي أمامَ السياطِ بحكمتِها

كلُّ موتٍ يُجذّرُني بالحياةِ

تشوعُ من الضربِ روحي، فأصعدُ

في السنديانِ الوريفِ

إلى آخر الأفقِ

هل تسمعين حفيفَ الغصونِ التي تتساقطُ...

هل تسمعين رفيفَ البراعمِ تُزهرُ...

هل تسمعينَ... ني ني ني ني ني ني

بأفواهِهم

يمضغونَ... ني ني ني ني ني ني ني ني

ني ني ني ني ني ني ني ني

وهم يحتسونَ النبيذَ الفرنسيَّ

كان المُفَوَّضُ ينقلُ عينيهِ

بين الأضابيرِ

والزرِّ

يزبدُ محتدماً

– أكنتَ تخطُّ الشعاراتِ ضِدَّ الوطن؟

– الحكومةُ ليستْ وطن

– ...

– ...

– خائن

– ...

120

as it sleeps, starved as a rusty bell.

From the flour of bombs,

  we make the delicious bread of life,

    and we milk the mirage.

My wounds are walled by crystal

shining with wisdom in front of the whips.

All deaths root me in life.

My soul flares up from the beatings. So I climb

    the leafy oak

      to the end of the horizon.

Do you hear the falling branches whispering?

Do you hear the budding buds shimmering?

Do you hear *me me me me me me*

    in their mouths,

they chew *me me me me me me me me me*

me me me me me me me me me

    while they sip French wine.

The investigating officer was glancing

    between my files

    and the bell.

Spit dribbles from his mouth:

– *Were you painting banners against the nation?*

– *The government is not the nation.*

– ...

– ...

– *Traitor!*

– ...

وفي باحةِ البيتِ، كان أخوهُ مسجّىً

– جبان

وخمسُ ر ر ر رصا صا صا صا صا صات

ت

ت

ت

ت

يلمعنَ في الصدرِ، مثلَ النجومِ المضيئة

–

...

... كان ليلُ المدينةِ يهمي نجوماً من الدمعِ

تلمعُ في حلكِ النائحاتِ

أمامَ القبورِ التي اندرستْ فاستحالَ الترابُ خدوداً

مخمّشةً بأناملهنَّ الرقيقةِ.

تمسحُها العجلاتُ التي عبرتْ بالمدافعِ

في غبشِ الفجرِ نحوَ القرى

فتطايرتِ الشجراتُ – البيوتُ

حمائمَ مذبوحةً

في الفضاءِ – الضريحِ...

[وأنتَ

على الأرضِ، بينهمُ، كُرَّةٌ تتقاذفُها الركلاتُ،

فتبصقُ عمرَكَ

فوقَ بلاطِ الزنازين،

سِنّاً،

فسِنّاً...

فما بين موتٍ وموتٍ،

مسافةُ أنْ تعترفْ...]

His brother lies in the courtyard of the house

– *Coward!*

Five bullets

      s

      s

      s

      s

      were twinkling like stars on his chest.

– …

…

The city night was dropping star-tears,

shining in the darkness of women weeping

in front of flattened graves; and the dirt became cheeks scratched by their

gentle fingers.

Tanks carrying artillery erased all trace

      while rumbling at dawn through the villages.

The trees/houses flew

      like wounded doves

      in the shrine/space…

{And you

are like a ball being kicked around on the ground.

So you spit out your age

      on the cell floor –

      one tooth

      after another.

Between one death and another,

      there is a space only to confess….}

– ألا تعترف...

يا ابنَ منيوكةِ الـ....!؟

...

كثيرون خانوا وأنتَ وراء المتاريس تشتلُ صبرَك

صبَيرةً في العراءِ. تُدخّنُك الحربُ سيجارةً تورّثُ من

عقبِ سيجارةٍ في فمِ العقداءِ؟،

تدافعُ عن شجرٍ لمْ تلامسْ شفاهُك خضرتَهُ،

وشوارعٍ لمْ تنتشِ بمباهجِها.

قلتُ: لا بأسَ روحي مُفخّخةٌ بالحقولِ.

سأفتحُ شبّاكَها

وأرى كيفَ تندلعُ السنبلاتُ – الحياةُ

الحياةُ. الحياةُ. **الحياةُ**. الحياةُ

الحياةُ. **الحياةُ**. الحياةُ

الحياةُ. الحياةُ. **الحياةُ** على بُعْدِ نبضٍ

ونافذةٍ من مكاتيبهم

فلماذا رموني هنا في الخنادقِ كالفأرِ أقرضُ خيطاً

سيُوصِلُني للنهايةِ.

هلْ نكتفي بالإجازاتِ مسروقةٍ لنقولَ بأنّا ارتكبنا الحياةَ.

أفي وسعِ زرقةِ هذا المدى أن تُبلّلَ روحي؟

أنُمسكُ كفَّ الفتاةِ لنرعشَ عامين من شهوةِ الحبِّ؟

هل عمرُنا غلطٌ يَتَعَقَّبُ خطوَ المُصحِّحِ للبارِ؟

أطفالُنا غلطٌ

والسنونُ التي سقطتْ قبلَ أسنانِنا غلطٌ.

حالِماً

في المقاهي

أصيدُ الشرودَ

ورائحةَ العابراتِ

– Won't you confess,

you son of a bitch?

...

Many betray. And you are behind the barricades, planting your patience,

a cactus in the wilderness. The war smokes you like a cigarette lit from

dog-ends in the colonels' mouths.

You defend the tree whose greenness your lips have never touched,

and the streets whose delights you've never enjoyed.

I said: *That's ok, my soul is brimming with fields.*

I will open her window

and see the ripening corn/life

life life life life

    life life life

       life life life is a short space from the pulse

       and the windows of their offices.

Why did they leave me in the trenches like a mouse chewing a thread

that will lead me to the end.

Is stolen military leave enough to say we have committed life?

Can this blue horizon wet my soul?

Do we have to hold a girl's palm to have a two-year orgasm?

Is our age as wrong as following the steps of the proof reader to the bar?

Are our kids mistakes?

    And are the years that fall out before our teeth do – mistakes?

Day dreaming

in cafés,

I snare the straying minds

and scent of women passing by,

ولكنَّ هذي الغيومَ التي شتَّتني على شفتيكِ
أضاعتْ خطى القلبِ
بين القصيدةِ والسجنِ...
هذي جروحُك أكثر مِمَّا نُعدُّ، ... ويبتسمُ الندلُ:
– كانت هنا في انتظارِكَ...

لي وطنٌ ضيَّعتهُ الحروبُ
ولي امرأةٌ شتَّتها الدروبُ
ولي حسرةٌ في الرياحِ تلوبُ...
فمِنْ أين ألتمُّ في وجعي – يا سياطُ –
إذا ازرقَّ جلدي،
وشفَّ سماءً لها كلُّ هذي النجومِ الموشّاةِ
تَكشِطُ عن روحيَ الصدأ المتقرّنَ...
...
– سوفَ أُريكَ نجومَ النهارِ
– ... –
رأيتُ النجومَ تلامسُ روحي،
وأصعدُ محتقناً بالعذاباتِ
نحوَ الإلهِ،...
أُريهِ المساميرَ في جسدي..
– تفْ...
– ... –
...
أُريدُ من الله موتاً نظيفاً
وداليةً فوقَ قبري
أشدُّ الأسى وتراً فترنُّ الرياحُ
... ولمْ أكترثْ

126

but these clouds, that dispersed me on your lips,

    have lost the steps of the heart

        between the poem and prison…

These are your countless wounds…And the waiters smile:

– *She was here, waiting for you…*

I have a country the wars wasted;

    and I have a woman the roads dispersed;

        and I have a sorrow spinning in the wind…

how do I gather in my grief, O whips,

        when my body has turned blue,

and when it shimmers like a sky embroidered with stars

        that scrape the corrosive rust off my soul…

…

– I will show you the stars at midday.

– …

I have seen the stars touching my soul,

       and I rise, contorted in pain,

            to God…

to show Him the nails in my body.

– *Tfuuh* (gobbing)

– …

…

I ask God for a clean death

and a vine over my grave.

I tighten sorrow like a tendon and the winds tinkle…

           …and I don't care.

ما الذي سوفَ يعني القتيلَ المُسَجَّى على الأرضِ شكلُ المسدَّسِ
مَنْ حضروا لجنازتِهِ؟
ما الذي سوف يعنيهِ لونُ الأكاليلِ
(..عَبُّودُ خطبوا لهُ مَرَّةً، هيهْ، هيهْ، هيهْ...
مِنْ غيرِ حمرةٍ محمَّرةٍ، هيهْ.. هيهْ.. هيـ....)
– ستزوعُ بأسمائِهم...
أو تزوعُ المصارينَ

–   ...

من فتحةٍ بين كُدْسٍ بساطيرِهم،
يَتَدَلَّى الفضاءُ على شكلٍ مِشنقةٍ...

زاعني فتخثَّرتُ
فوقَ البلاطِ
وما لَمَّني أحدٌ...
ما لهم كلَّما عبروني،
أشاحوا بأعينِهم...

...

في الطريقِ، لعينيكِ
أوقفني الرجلُ الجمركيُّ
وفتَّشَ قلبي ومحفظتي...
لمْ يكنْ في دمي غيرُ خارطةٍ للعذاباتِ
لمْ ترَها عينهُ الزئبقيَّةُ
– واللهِ، يا سيِّدي أنَّها صورتي
ناحلٌ كالقطاراتِ في البردِ
مُتَّشحٌ بالتشرّدِ والمفرداتِ اللعينةِ
... يا ليتها تَعْرِفُ الآنَ أيَّ المخاوفِ تقتسمُ القلبَ – هذا المجوّفَ – هذا المجوّفَ، كالطبلِ –
هذا الكسيرَ أمامَ وجومِ المفوَّضِ...

128

What does the murdered man care, laid out on the ground like a pistol?

Who attended his funeral?

What does the colour of the wreaths mean to him?

(Aboud just got engaged to a woman, *ladi di dadi da*. She's so beautiful,

she doesn't need make up, *ladi dadi da*...)

– You will vomit their names...

    or you will throw up your insides.

– ...

From a hole in a heap of their boots...

the space dangles like a scaffold.

He vomited me, and I clotted

on the floor.

No one collected me.

Each time they pass,

    they just turn their eyes away...

...

On my way to your eyes

the customs officer stopped me,

and searched my heart and my wallet...

There was nothing in my blood but a map of inflictions

that his capricious eyes didn't spot.

– *I swear to God, sir, it's my picture,*

thin as trains in the cold,

and wrapped in homelessness and damned vocabulary.

...I wish she knew what fears divide the heart now – this hollow drum,

struck dumb before the silence of the commissioned officer.

– واللهِ يا سيِّدي أنّها...

كان وجهي خلاصةَ جوعِ المدينةِ

كان صديقَ الكلابِ التي قاسمتني فُتَاتَ المزابلِ والبردِ

ها أنني أعرفُ الناسَ والأثرياءَ المرابين – يا سيِّدي – واحداً، واحداً،

من خلالِ امتلاءِ مزابلِهم...

أعرفُ الآن

أيَّ اللحومِ، يُفضِّلُ هذا المفوَّضُ...

...

...

كان بيني، وبين المفوَّضِ،

طاولةٌ للحوارِ العقيمِ

وزرٌّ...

ومن خلفِ نافذةٍ مسدلةٍ

كنتُ أسمعُ ليلَ المدينةِ يَعوي كذئْبٍ جريحٍ يُمرِّغُهُ الجوعُ في قفصٍ،

والشوارعَ منسيَّةً بين أدراجِهِ. بين ظلِّ السما

والزجاجةِ ظلُّ القتيلِ الذي كان يَكبُرُ

في خطواتِ المصابيحِ والخوذِ السودِ، يمتدُّ، يمتدُّ،...

تقطعُهُ السرفاتُ ولا أحدٌ في المدينةِ غيرُ

الجنودِ يشيلونَ آثائَنا كالغبارِ بأكمامِهم.

كربلاء – يبوس – سراييفو، بأجراسِها كبغالٍ مطقَّمةٍ.

المكانُ هو الإرثُ.

لا أرضَ لي

أتعثَّرُ بين الزنازينِ والناطحاتِ

وأسقُطُ بين صدى طلقةٍ وندى زهرةٍ، تتفتَّتُ تحتَ تخوتِ

الحدائقِ. كلُّ سماءٍ أكوِّرُها في يدي

سوفَ تفلِتُ مني كرملِ الشواطيءِ (... تنحدرُ القطراتُ: تُ، تك، تك، تُ، تُ تك،

تك، تك، تك، تك،

130

– I swear to God, sir, it's...

My face was a summary of the city's famine,

a friend to the dogs that share the cold and rubbish-tip scraps.

I know the people and the rich usurers, sir, every one,

      from the size of their overstuffed bins.

I know now

what type of meat the commissioned officer prefers...

...

...

There was a table between me and the commissioned officer,

      a table for idle chat,

and a button.

And from behind the closed window

I heard the city night howling like a wounded wolf rolling in its cage

while the streets lie forgotten in his desk. Between the shadow of the sky

and the window, the shadow of the murder victim grew and extended

in the wake of the street lamps and black helmets

      until the tanks tracked through it. No one in the city but

      soldiers carrying our furniture like dust on their sleeves.

      Karbala, Yabous, – Sarajevo – their bells like a gang of mules.

      This place is their heritage,

but no land for me.

Stumbling between cells and skyscrapers

I fall between the echo of a bullet and the dew of a flower smashed in

the gardens. Each sky that I cup in my hand

will drip off me like sand, drip drip drip drip

drip drip drip drip drip

131

تُ، تك،

تك،

تـ.

ك

...

كما إبرٌ في السكونِ تُمزِّقُ ررررررر..ﷺﷺﷺﷺﷺﷺاسـ.. سـ.. سي.
أُروِّضُ جسمي لأقصى العذاباتِ، كي يستمرَّ أمامَ السياطِ

امنحيني ولو قطرةً من شرابِكِ
يا كاردوين لأُبصِرَ أبوابَ سيبيل أين ستفضي؟...
الراباتُ تَنبُتُ بين أصابعنا طُرقاً ليسَ نعرفُها
صاحَ أقدَمُنا في السجونِ:
أهينوا بأجسادِكم تصمدوا)

لن يعودَ لنا الكزُزُ... عَبُودُ
روحي مُعلَّقةٌ من غلاصيمِها.
أنتشي بالورودِ،
فيصعدُ في رئتي المستفزَّةِ رائحةُ البولِ (... اعتني بحديقةِ
روحي، إذا متُّ) لا تتركوا الكتبَ والضوءَ قربَ ضريحي أنا
تعبٌ وأريدُ أنامَ[60]. يقولُ لي النايُ ما لا تقولُ الرياحُ.
زفيرُ الطبيعةِ هذي البراكينُ[61]. أينَ زفيرُكَ يا صاحبي؟
خذْ صليبَكَ واتبعني. أنُفتِّشُ عن موتِنا لا
نراه؟... ونرغبُ فيه فيهربُ بين أصابعِنا[62]... كانَ آخرُ ما
قالهُ في الملفِّ: لماذا الغموضُ وقاتلُنا واضحُ،
واضحٌ كالمسدَّسِ في رئةٍ زفرتْ كلَّ أرجائِها في الخزانةِ، أو غامضٌ
كالخزانةِ في غرفةِ البنتِ، علَّقتُ صبري بمشجبِها
ومضيتُ... (أُعَلِّقُ في مشجبِ السوطِ جلدي الممزَّقَ مِّشحاً بالملفَّاتِ،

132

drip drip

drip

dri

d

…

Like needles in the silence tearing up my headddddddddddddddddd,
I train my body to endure pain so it can withstand the whips.

O Cassandra, give me a drop of your potion

      to open the doors of the Sybil. Where will they lead to?

    Flutes will sprout unknown roads from our fingers.

The oldest prisoner shouted:

Stand tall and strong to survive!

The cherry will not come back to us…Aboud,
my soul is hung by its gills.

    I get high on roses

      until the smell of piss irritates my lungs (…take care of my soul's
garden when I die). Don't leave books and a light near my shrine, I'm
tired and I want to sleep.[60] The flute says what the wind doesn't say.
These volcanoes are nature's exhalations.[61] Where is yours, my friend?
Take your cross and follow me. Do we search for our death and not find
it? We crave it when it runs through our fingers.[62] The last thing he said
was: *Why the mystery when our killer is crystal clear?*
Clear like a bomb in the lung that exploded in the closet, or mysterious
like the closet in a girl's room. I hung my patience on her peg and
left…(I hang my torn skin on a whip-rack, covered with files…

أماهُ لِمْ جئتِ بي للشجونِ. كمرآتِها
وهي تندبُ وحدَتها في الظلامِ
ولا قمرٍ فوقَ قضبانِ نافذتي أو يداكِ...
لشدّةِ يأسي أضئتُكِ،
هلْ أخسرُ الأرضَ كي أريحَ القبرَ،
نمشي وثالثنا الهجرُ)
عمّنْ يوضِّحُ لي شهوتي لصقَ ساقيكِ،
منفرجَين على مقعدٍ عابرٍ،
لأرى كيف تزلقُ
عيني،
فأرفعُها للكتابِ... (فأزلقُ فوقَ برازٍ قديمٍ
يفتّتهُ الدودُ، أنهضُ متسخاً لاعناً)
أيّ مزبلةٍ تسعُ الأرضَ...
[يبصقُ عَبُودٌ في الدودِ يحملُ أسلابَهُ. كلُّ تاريخِنا
صدفةٌ يقتضيها
السياقُ...]
احتذاني وسازَ يفاصلُني بلباقتِهِ عن أساي بشتَّى الشروحاتِ،
شتَّى نُصفِّقُ في البرلمانِ عن الفولِ
والوحدةِ الوطنيّةِ. أضرطُ أضرطُ...
أضرطُ[63]، فوقَ مدارِ حياتي بكلِّ
قواي... (أرى الدودَ يدنو،
فأبعدُ ماعونَنا عن غلاصمِهِ)
سرقتنا الشوارعُ من ظلِّنا في الشوارعِ.
لمْ يكنِ الوهمُ أبعدَ من ضحكاتِ الصخورِ عن البحرِ غيَّبها
في التماهي تنفّسُ أحلامِها في الرمالِ على لغةٍ علستها البلاغةُ ثمَّ رمتها على
فمِنا كالنفاياتِ. ما عمرهُ زيدُ البحرِ؟ ما ثقلهُ؟
ناتفاً ريشَ ماعت[64] لكي أزنَ الظلمَ تحتَ بساطيرِهم

134

Mum, why was I born to sadness? Like her mirror

       while she sobs, lonely in the dark.

No moon on the bars of my window, or on your hands…

too much of my sorrow lights you up.

    Do I have to lose the earth to win the grave?

     We walk together with a companion – loss.)

     Who will explain to me my orgasm near your legs,

   wide open as I passed the bench,

    or how

       my eyes slide,

      and I raise them to the book…(I slip over on old excrement

      guzzled by worms. I stand up, dirty and cursing).

      What rubbish bin can hold the earth…?

[Aboud is spitting on the worms that carry his rags. All our history is

    chance dictated

    by context].

He made me into shoes and walked, banging on about my sorrows,

     and how in parliament we applaud stewed beans

     and national unity. I fart, fart…

       fart,[63] above the horizon of my life with all the

       strength that I have…(I see worms approaching

    and I push our dish away from them).

    The street stole us from our own shadow in the street.

   The illusion was nothing more than rocks laughing by the sea, lost

in dreams, breathing a language chewed by rhetoric, then dumped in our

mouths like garbage. How old is the foam of the sea? How heavy is it?

I pluck the feathers of Maat[64] to weigh the injustice under their boots

تزنُ الأرضَ كوَّرها إلتجرا[65] على قدمٍ كالنعامةِ

تسبقُنا نظرةٌ قتلتْ جوجوليانَ[66] كيفَ مضى

بين هام وزا فوق بغلتِهِ تيلبينو الكسيح إلى جرحِنا

سوَّرتهُ لقدموس[67] أسنانُ تنِّين تمتدُّ من عصرٍ هسيود

حتى حذاءِ الرئيسِ المبطَّنِ بالفروِ والغزوِ:

يا سيِّدي، لا ذرائعَ تحتاجُها (تتفجَّرُ أجسادُنا مثلَ بالونةٍ تحتَ

كرباجِهِ، وهو يضحكُ منتشياً) امتلا ثورُ فاليس

من لحمِ صرْخاتِنا

رافعين بأقداحِهم نشوةً لخوارِ المدينةِ:

كومود[68]

هليوجالا[69]

مكسيما[70]

نيرون

هتلر... الخ

جنكيز خان

سيموزا

هولاكو

يونغ لو[71]

كاليكولا... الخ

القائدُ الأوحدُ، الرمزُ

القائدُ الفذُّ

– نعم سيِّدي[72]

الجميعُ يقولُ: نعم سيِّدي...

الواحدُ، الأحدُ، الصمدُ، الفردُ، يُغْني، ويُفْني، يُميتُ،

ويُحْيِي، و...[73]

that anchor the earth orbited by Altjira[65] with the feet of an ostrich.

A glance that preceded us has killed Cú Chulainn.[66] How did Tilibino reach our wounds on the back of his mule; and how were our wounds for Cadmus[67] fenced in by dragon teeth from the time of Hesiod.

Even the president's shoes, stuffed with fur and invasion:
Sir, you don't need excuses (our bodies explode like a balloon under his whip, and he is excited, laughing). The iron bull of Phallus is full with the flesh of our cries.
They raise their cups to toast the bawling of the city:
Comodo[68]

    Heliogala[69]

        Maxima[70]

            Nero

                Hitler...etc.

Genghis Khan

    Simoza

  Hulago

    Yang Lu[71]

        Caligula...etc.

One leader, the symbol,
the smartest leader
– *Yes, sir.*[72]

Everybody says: *Yes, sir...*
The one, the eternal, the one, donating, annihilating, killing,
reincarnating, and...[73]

(النفاياتُ تعلو على لغتي

ما أقلَّ القصيدة!

خمسونَ ألف قتيلٍ على الأرضِ

لم يبكِهمْ أحدُ)[74]

القذيفةُ في السبطانةِ، ماذا إذاً يلدُ الغدُ

... أو يَعِدُ[75]

وما نحنُ إلّا حجارُ الطواحينِ.

اقلبوا أرضَنا حجراً حجراً،[76]

تجدوا دمَنا راعفاً...

آهِ من أمّةٍ لا تعيشُ بدون حروبٍ،

فإنْ خَرجتْ من ليالي البسوسِ، مضتْ لحروبِ البنوكِ،

فأنْ بدأ القصفُ غطّتْ على رأسِها الرملَ.

ليتكَ قلتَ بأنّا نحاربُ هذا الهواءَ ليعبرَ جندُ التتارِ،

على جُثّتي، كي يُقيموا لأهلي مأدبةً للسلامِ

....

....

....

وكنّا سنبقَّى نُعمِّرُ هذي البلادَ

كما شاءَها الربُّ في حُلمِهِ البابليِّ

جِنَاناً مُعلَّقَةً، يَتَرَقْرقُ فوقَ مدارجِها الماءُ والصلواتُ

ولكنَّهم هدمونا

أشادوا على دمِنا المتيبِّسِ، زنزانةً

وادَّعوا أنّها وطنٌ

ثمَّ قالوا: هنيئاً بما يخصبُ البلدُ

138

(Garbage accumulates over my language.

How small is the poem!

Fifty thousand dead men on the earth,

and no one cried for them).[74]

The artillery shell is in the barrel. What will the future give birth to?

What will it promise?[75]

We were only millstones.

Dig our ground stone by stone,[76]

and you will find our fresh blood.

What nation can't live without wars!

When they end the Basus war, they start a war with the banks.

When the bombing starts they will bury their heads in the sand.

If only you'd said we could tilt at air so the Tartar soldiers can march

on my body and host a celebration for peace.

....

....

....

We would have gone on building these lands

as God wanted in his Babylonian dream –

water and prayers rippling over the steps of its hanging gardens

but they destroyed us,

built a prison from our dried blood

and called it a homeland

then said: *Be grateful for your country.*

...

لا بحرَ نثلمُهُ بالمراكبِ

يا أيّها النائمون على حَجرِ الثورةِ المستحيلةِ

لا رمل أو زيدُ

رأيتُ دمي في الطوابعِ يلصقُها المبعدونَ...

إلى أينَ تسعى بنفسِكَ؟

إنَّ الحياةَ — البلادَ التي تبتغي...

....

....

....

مَحْضُ أغانٍ تفرّشُ أسنانَها في وضوحِ الكلامِ

أعَلّقُ نفسي على جذعِ ياكِ لأقطفَ ذكراكِ.

كورماك [77] لا تُظْهِرِ الآنَ كأسَكَ

أينَ مضى الشعراءُ؟

يَسوطُهمُ الخوفُ نحوَ كهوفِ الغُمُوضِ

وكلبُهمْ باسطٌ ذيلَهُ بالوصيدِ [78]

الجليدُ يُغطِّي المديَدَ

وأقْصِدُ: كمْ جُلدوا؟ من بعيدٍ، أرى من بعيدٍ،

ظلالَ المدينةِ والحافلاتِ التي تحشرُ الصيفَ والفتياتِ الجميلاتِ

في كأسِهِ (ما الذي سوفَ يعنيكَ؟

ماذا سيعني السجينَ اخضرارُ السهولِ)

....

....

....

140

...

No sea for us to slice with boats

O you that sleep on the stones of the impossible revolution,

                    no sand or foam:

I saw my blood in the stamps stuck on by deportees...

      Where are you wandering to by yourself?

      Life is – the land that you seek....

....

....

....

Just as the song brushes her teeth to clean her speech,

I hang myself from Yggdrasil to pick at your memories.

Hide the grail, Cormac.[77]

Where did the poets go?

Whipped by fear towards the caves of ambiguity

      while their dog wagged his tail at the entrance.[78]

The snow is covering the ground

but I mean: how much were they whipped? From a distance I see the

shadows of the city and buses that hustle summer and its beautiful girls

into a glass of wine (what does that matter to you?

What do green fields mean to the prisoner?)

....

....

....

سأرجعُ من وطنِ النفيِّ بعدَ ثلاثين عاماً
لأُطْرُقَ بابَ البلادِ بعُكَّازِ شيخوختي –
مَنْ ستفتحُ للكهلِ سيقانَها؟
وأُقْصِدُ عمراً يسيرُ بعُكَّازةٍ
ما الذي ظلَّ منهُ؟)... يرفعُهُ نخبَ غربتِهِ
فيرى حزنَهُ طافياً كالفراتِ،
على رغوةِ الخمرِ

. . . .

. . . .

. . . .

يكرهُها ظامئاً فَتَفِرُّ خطى الفتياتِ سراعاً إلى تخمةِ
الزوجِ، مرَّ هو الزوجُ بالبُنِّ تَلْعَقُهُ فتسيلُ على شفتيها
لزوجةُ مُكرِ الرجالِ وطعمُ السجائرِ (تمضي البناتُ إلى
السُكرِ في آخر الحبِّ،
نمضي إلى الشِعرِ في أولِ الحبِّ، نرمي
فحولاتِنا كالحصى في اختلاطِ المياهِ) إلى أين يمتدُّ
خيطُ زفيري،[79] يا مواري،
بين القصيدةِ
والقصدِ.
ترزمُني الطرقاتُ وترسلُني في بريدِ الدموع إليها
(– الرجالُ هم غرفٌ لانتظارِكِ) تضحكُ حين تراني
أغلّفُ قلبي بكيسِ البلاهةِ، مرتبكاً مثل طيرٍ
تَعَلَّقَ في الشوكِ (– لا عاشقٌ جاهزٌ في الحقيبةِ،
يصلحُ للحفلاتِ الأنيقةِ) سيِّدتي، الطيورُ تنوحُ على شجري،
وتُغنِّي على فننِ الآخرين (– أقلبُك قبري؟...)

142

I'll return from exile after thirty years

       to knock on the door of my country with an old man's stick –

       who will open her legs to an old man?

       I mean that age, walking with a stick,

what's left of it?…It is raised like a toast to exile,

so he sees his sadness flooding like the Euphrates

on a foam of alcohol.

…………………………

…………………………

…………………………

He gulps it thirstily, and the girls run away fast to their rapacious

husband, the husband is bitter as coffee. She licks it and onto her lips

flows his tacky deceitfulness and the taste of cigarettes, and the girls walk

away to get drunk when love ends.

At the beginning of love, we walk away to poetry, we throw away our

masculinity like pebbles in the raging water. O you Fates, how far will

the thread of my breath stretch,[79] O Mowari,

between poetry

and its meaning?

The roads packaged me and sent me through the mournful mail to her

(men have become waiting rooms for you) she laughs when she sees me,

covering my heart with a bag of stupidity, feeling awkward like a bird

strangled in thorns (there is no lover waiting in the bag,

       fit for a ritzy party). My lady, the birds are weeping on my tree,

       but they sing in the gardens of others (is your heart my grave?)

لقد تركتني أهشُّ قطيعَ مدامعِها

عن مروجِ جنوني.

كأنْ لمْ يكنْ بيننا والحجونِ

أنيسٌ سوى...

فوّضتني الدروبُ إليكِ، أضيعُ وراءَكِ في كلِّ خطوٍ[80]... إلى
أين أمضي، أنا، رجلٌ ليسَ لي في يدي غيرُ عشرِ أناملَ،
لم تتهجَّ سوى الكلماتِ وجسمِكِ. أيُّ جحيمٍ، إلهي، سأرضى
سوى هجرِها. أيُّ دُكّانِ تبغٍ صغيرٍ أبيعُ به.

أيُّ شيءٍ سأرضاهُ غيرَ عذابِ الكتابةِ[81]

(أغلقُ بابي وأحكمُ فيها الرتاجَ

بسلسلةِ السنواتِ المريرةِ) نحنُ الجميلين في الموتِ،
أكثرُ مَوْتاً من الوردِ.

....

....

....

تنامُ على حُلمٍ بالفجرِ...

ولكنَّ الفجرَ بعيدٌ...

ما زالَ وراءَ القضبانْ

رأيتُ: القمرَ الناعسَ يحملُهُ الحوتُ بفكَّيهِ،

فنهزجُ فوق التنكاتِ:

"يا حوتتنا البلّاعهْ، ردي گمرنا بساعهْ"

لكنَّ الحوتَ غدا ديناصوراً،

والقمرَ المبلوعَ تناساهُ الصبيانْ

ونحن يُجمِّعُنا المنفى وتُفرِّقُنا الأوطانْ

فمَنْ يُنشِدُ للإنسانِ المكسوفِ الخاطرِ لحنَ تَغَرُّبِهِ في بطنِ الإنسانْ

144

She left me herding the herds of her tears,

far from my crazy meadows

as if there was no distance between us and Al-Hujun,

sociable, but...

The roads take me to you, I get lost behind you in every step.[80] Where

do I go? I'm a man, I have nothing on my hand but ten fingers which

can't spell anything but words and your body. My God, I can accept any

hell except her abandonment. I'll work in any small tobacco store,

I'll accept anything but the torture of writing.[81]

(I close the door and lock it

with a chain of bitter years.) We are beautiful in death,

more dead than flowers...

....

....

....

You sleep and dream about dawn

but dawn is very far away –

it's still behind bars:

I saw the sleepy moon being carried in the jaws of a whale.

We sing while beating empty cans –

O whale, swallower, return our moon quickly!

But the whale turned into a monster –

the swallowed moon has been forgotten by children.

Exile unites us, our homeland divides us.

So who sings to sad humanity the song of forgiveness we carry inside us?

....

....

....

هابطاً في دروبِ المدينةِ يبحثُ عن سببٍ مقنعٍ

لانتفاخِ كروشِ الطغاةِ بعصرِ المجاعاتِ...

(أسمعُ خلفي: نحيبَ العصورِ يدبُّ بحقلِ العظامِ وما خلَّفَ الدودُ

من جِيَفٍ وأضاحٍ

وما مَلَّ جَلَّادُنا

ما مَلِلْنا

وما مَلَّتِ الأرضُ

....

....

....

هذي السيولُ التي لا تكفُّ عن الجريانِ إلى أين تذهبُ؟

هذي الدموعُ إلى أين؟) هذا الترابُ الذي تحتَنا من رفاتِ الجدودِ

فكيفَ تدوسُ عليه بساطيرُهمْ

دونَ أنْ تَصرُخَ الأرضُ

أصرخُ هذا المدى أرضُنا

كيف نَنْزِعُها من أظافِرِنا

كلُّ نسغٍ بأشجارِها كانَ ينبضُ من دِمِنا في عروقِ

الغصونِ الوريقةِ

يُزهِرُ...

هذا الغبارُ مثارُ سنابِكِنا في أديمِ الحضارةِ

هذا الضبابُ تحشرجُ أنفاسِنا في الممرِّ إلى صالةِ اللهِ

146

....

....

....

Falling onto the city roads, looking for a reason why

the tyrants' bellies are so big and bloated in a time of famine...

(I hear behind me the eras wail, crawling in a field of bones and worms'

excrement and carrion and sacrifices

    and our hangman wasn't bored yet

and we weren't bored

and the land wasn't bored.)

....

....

....

These everflowing torrents, where do they go?

Where do these tears go? The dust of our ancestors is still under our feet

so how do their boots step on it – how do they step on it

       without the ground crying out?

I shout: *This country is ours,*

      how can we clean it from under our nails?

Each part of its trees used to pulse from our blood to the veins of the

leafy branches,

flowering...

    this dust is raised, driven by centuries of civilisation.

    This fog lies heavy on our chests on the way to God's hall.

لامعةٌ بالكريستالِ أخطاؤُنا...
وحفيفُ الرياحِ البعيدةِ أصواتُ أسلافِنا
قادمون من الحجرِ الصلدِ...

....
....
....

صاعداً في النشيدِ
إلى قلبِ أوروك،
ألقي الظلالَ على وطنٍ لا ظلال لهُ
غيرُ ما خلَّفتهُ البنادقُ من بقعٍ وتماثيل
تأتي الفصولُ وتَذبُلُ
تأتي الجيوشُ وترحلُ
تأتي الملوكُ وتَبْقى..
يُشيِّدُ أحدُهم قلعةً من جماجِمنا
ليُهدِّمَها آخررررررر
ليُشيِّدَ برجَ حَمَامٍ
وكلٌّ له شاعِر رررررررررر
ومُؤرِّخ خ خ خ خ خ خ...

....
....
....

أصعدُ أسوارَ هذي المدينةِ
دكَّتْ معاقلَها الطائراتُ المغيرةُ

148

Our mistakes shine in the crystals

and the rustle of distant winds is the sound of our ancestors

coming from hard stone.

....

....

....

I am raised by the anthem

       to the heart of Uruk

I throw shadows in a country that has no shadows

except for the legacy left by an armoury of stains and statues.

Seasons come and fade away,

armies come and fade away,

kings come and stay…

one of them builds a castle from our skulls

while another and another destroys them

     to build a pigeon's nest

and each has a poet and a poet and a poet and a poet

      and a historian and a historian and a historian…

....

....

....

I climb the walls of the city

      trashed by enemy aircraft

أُبصِرُ ننكال[82] نافشةً شَعرَها

فوقَ أطلالِها وهي تشدو المراثي وتلطمُ

تكشطُها البلدوزراتُ،

ليبني المقاولُ فوق شواهدِها، وطناً من مصارف

تعلو

وتعلو (وقلبي يخافُ من المصعدِ الكهربائيِّ) تعلو المداخنُ

تعلو المنائرُ

تعلو المدافعُ

والزفراتُ الحبيسةُ – هذا السخامُ انشدادُ النشيدِ على قوسٍ أحلامِنا

سوفَ نُطْلِقُهُ في الفضاءِ الأخيرِ فيجفلُ في دمِنا مِخلَبٌ.

يتراءى له برجُ بابل

أسود

من زفراتِ المعاملِ

ينسلُّ طابوقةً إثْرَ طابوقةٍ

في المتاحفِ

ينهبُهُ البدوُ تحتَ عباءاتِهم

والحكوماتُ لمْ تنتبهْ

حارسُ البرجِ لمْ ينتبهْ

لمرورِ جلالتِهِ

وهو يسألُ عن عُشْبِ گلگامش...

– سيِّدي، أكلتهُ الخرافُ. أما كان أنفُكَ – عفوكَ –

يَنشِقُ خلفَ القطيعِ برازَ الـ....

– ...

لكنَّهُ قبلَ أنْ يستبينَ الحقيقةَ[83]

غطُّوهُ حتى مشارفِ عينيهِ

في جومةٍ للبرازْ...

150

and see Ninkal[82] with her hair spread

      over its ruins, lamenting as she beats herself.

Bulldozers scrape it off

so contractors can cover its tombs with banking districts.

      Above,

            above (and my heart is afraid of heights) above the chimneys

            above the minarets

                above the cannons –

                    the rancid breath of those trapped below dirties our

vision and launches it into space to be raked by bloody claws –

            and the tower of Babel becomes clear...

    smuts

      from the soot of factories

         soil the museum exhibits

pilfered by Bedouins under their djellabas

brick by brick

and governments don't notice

and the tower guard didn't notice

      his majesty passing.

        When he asks for Gilgamesh's plant –

– *Sir, it was eaten by a sheep, but wasn't it your nose, pardon me,*

          that was sniffing that pile of shit...

– ...

But before he could see into the depths[83]

they buried him in shit

      up to his eyeballs

فرأى

كلَّ

شيء...

...

[ولا شيء،

كانوا يحكُّون أسوارَ بابل

كي يضعوا صُوَرَ الجنرالِ

على كلِّ طابوقةٍ

ضحك الفأرُ حتى تبدَّتْ نواجذُهُ

عن مدائنَ لا تنتهي

وأشارَ بأذنيهِ نحوَ الطغاةِ الذين تلاشوا

على سُورِها المتطاولِ (أنتفُ لحيةً عرَّافِ بابل نتفاً

أما قلتَ لي: إنَّ كلَّ الغزاةِ

سيندحرون على بابِها...

ليتنا لمُ نُصدِّقْ سوى دمعِنا

يترقرقُ

فوقَ سفوحِ الجنائن

يسقي العصورَ

أما قلتَ لي:

إنَّ هذا الفراتَ

سيطغي

لمرأى دماءِ بنيهِ

على جرفِهِ

فيهيجُ

يُحطِّمُ

كلَّ السدودِ – الجسورِ

152

...and then

he saw

everything...

...

and nothing.

    They were scraping the walls of Babylon

        to put pictures of the General

            on every brick.

The mouse laughed until his back teeth

           turned into endless cities

and he pointed his ears towards the tyrants who had vanished

on their high walls; (I tugged the beard of the Babylonian fortune-teller.

Didn't you say to me that all invaders

        will be blocked by its door?

If only we could believe that our tears

        pouring

        over the slopes of mountains

           will quench the thirst of centuries.

Didn't you say to me

    that this Euphrates

      will flood

        at the sight of its sons' blood

      on its bank

    and will seethe

    and destroy

      all its dams – all its bridges?

فما بالهُ يتوقَّفُ منكسرَ العينِ،

قدَّامَ خيلِ يزيد[84]

يُلملِمُ أذيالَهُ خجلاً

عن قميصِ الحسينِ المُمزَّقِ بالطعناتِ

ويمضي ذليلاً إلى آخرِ الدهرِ والبحرِ)

يأتي الغزاةُ وراءَ الطغاةِ

ويأتي الطغاةُ وراءَ الغزاةِ

ولا شيءَ...

يستبدلونَ الغِلالَ، بأُخرى

السجونَ، بـ"أُخْـ.....ـر.....ا"

ويمضي بنا العمرُ،

جوعاً،

ونفياً،

وقهرا...

وهم راسخونَ على الأرضِ،

دهراً، فدهرا

....

....

....

نُباعُ ونُشرى

ولمْ ندرِ أمرا

ونُذبحُ مثل الشياهِ،

بساحِ معارِكِهمْ

كي يزيدوا حدودَ الممالكِ

شبرا

But why has it stopped, ashamed,

in front of Yazīd's [84] *horses —*

    pulling the edge of its bank away

        from Al-Hussein's shirt, ripped by stab wounds,

           and then going on, humiliated, to the end of time and to the sea?)

The invaders come after the tyrants,

the tyrants come after the invaders

and nothing happens...

they replace crops with other crops

and prisons with other...

and time stretches out

        in hunger

           exile

                and oppression

while the oppressors keep on going,

generation after generation.

....

....

....

We are bought and sold

with no say

like sheep slaughtered

        on the battlefield

      so they can extend their borders

          by a hand-span.

....

....

....

أنامُ وأصحو، فلا أجدُ الفجرَ.

مَنْ سرقَ الفجرَ – يا ديكُ – من شُرفاتِ المدينةْ...

....

....

....

أأقضي على وحشتي بالكتابةِ؟

لكنْ إلى مَ؟ أقولُ لگلگامش:

لو رأيتَ

الذي

قد

رأينا

لبلتَ على رأسِ هذي الحياةِ

وأسألُ: هل عمرُنا سجنُنا؟

هل كتابي ضريحي؟

هل أرى البابَ حُلماً أنامُ لأدخلَهُ؟

هل أجرّبُ موتي لعلّي أرى عالماً

لمْ يصوّرهُ ملتون

أُخرِجُ رأسي بين السطورِ لأُبصِرَ:

أطفالَنا يلعبونَ بميراثِنا

من حقولِ القنابلِ

156

....

....

....

I sleep and wake, but I can't find morning –
who stole it – O cockerel on the city balconies...?

....

....

....

How long must I cure my loneliness with writing?
I say to Gilgamesh:

>   *If*
>
>   *you saw*
>
>   *what*
>
>   *we've seen*
>
>   *you'd have pissed on life.*

And I ask: *Is our life our prison?*
Is my book my grave?
Is the door a dream for me to go through?
Did I risk death to glimpse a parallel world
>   *beyond Milton's imagining?*

I lift my head from the lines to see
>   children playing with our legacy –

>   fields of bombs

والفتياتِ على نهرِ دجلة
يغسلنَ أوجهَهنَّ
فتمضي المياهُ مُرقرقةً بالجمالِ ليكرعَها البحرُ
كمْ كرعَ البحرُ أحلامَنا
جالسون على حجرِ الحِكْمةِ البابليَّةِ

....
....
....

أحتاجُ عمراً أضيفُ إليهِ نبيذَكِ...
أكنسُ باحةَ بيتي من الحربِ والفضلاتِ،
أقولُ انتظرتُكِ حتى تبرعمَ
– في فرجةِ البابِ –
غُصْنُ التلهُّفِ
وأمتدَّ بين عيوني وبين غيابِكِ غاباً كثيفاً.
لماذا أضعتُكِ، سيِّدتي، في زحامِ القصيدةِ
(أُبصِرُها خلفَ واجهةِ الحانِ،
تضحكُ، تُمسِكُ خيطَ دموعي
وتسحبُني) كلّما مرَّتِ الطائراتُ
تذكّرتُ ليلى المريضةَ
فوقَ سفوحِ العراقِ
يحاصرُها الثلجُ والمدفعيُّون...

أزحفُ بين القبورِ وألغامِنا، فأُحِسُّ دبيبَ
أغانيكِ خافتةً في صفيرِ الرياحِ تهدهدُ ليلَ
القرى الغافياتِ

158

and young girls by the Tigris

        washing their faces

           so their beauty drains away to be drunk by the sea –

how many of our dreams did the sea drink

as we sat on the timeless stones of Babylonian wisdom?

      . . . .

      . . . .

      . . . .

I need a lifetime to add your wine to –

        sweeping the war and crap out of the courtyard of my house,

    I said: *I wait for you*

  in the doorway

        until the branch of longing buds

and then, between my eyes and your absence, grows into a jungle.

Why did I lose you, love, in a crowd of poems

(I see her on the other side of the pub,

    she laughs, catches my thread of tears

        and draws me near) whenever the airplanes pass

I remember Layla, who is sick

    in the Iraqi foothills,

      besieged by snow and gunners…

I crawl between the graves and our mines, sensing the tread of your soft

songs subdued beneath the whistle of a wind that lulls the nights of

sleeping villages

(ثيابي مُبلَّلةٌ بنديفِ الغيومِ. وقلبي ملاذُ العصافيرِ.

هل تَلمسين به الزغبَ الحلوَ ينمو جناحاً من اللهفةِ المستحيلةِ،

علّي أطيرُ، أطيرُ...

إلى وطني، لأراكِ) ولنْ أستعيرَ جناحَ

القطا[85]، دجَّنتهُ المدينةُ.

قلتُ: انتظرتُكِ غيماً حزيناً يمرُّ على شُرفةِ القلبِ يغسلُ

حقلَ الرمادِ الذي خلَّفتهُ المدافعُ (ألقيتُ ظلّي على البحرِ،

مُنقسماً في السفائنِ تمخرُ بي نحوَ دلمون[86]

فاضطربَ البحرُ من لغتي

تاركاً عبقاً أزرقاً من دموعي على العُشبِ.

مرَّ الربيعُ وما زالَ قلبي سجينَ الوريقاتِ صفراءَ

يكنسُها الريحُ فوقَ سطورِ الحدائقِ)

أصعدُ من وجعِ الأرضِ. أحفرُ لوحاً من الطينِ:

لا فجرَ أجملُ من شمسِ حُرِّيتي

يومَ نكسرُ قضبانَنا وندقُّ على بابِ قصرِ الطواغيتِ

(يساقطُ الشعراءُ على دبقِ المهرجاناتِ. أنهضُ مكتئباً،

صافقاً، خلفيَ البابَ

أختارُ باراً بعيداً.

أكشُّ طنينَ القوافي،

وأحْلُمُ بالبحرِ، أزرقَ ينسابُ تحتَ جفوني.

أسيرُ وحيداً على الرملِ خلفَ خطاكِ

ولا أصلُ...) البحرُ عاتٍ بأمواجِهِ والجراذينُ

تأكلُ من سفني

وأنا أتصارعُ والموجَ – رَبّاهُ –

لا وطنٌ في السفينةِ.

أنهضُ من رغوةِ الكأسِ،

لا شيءَ غيرُ خطى الجندِ والرملِ...

160

(my clothes wet with clouds and my heart a haven for finches.

Do you feel the soft down growing into a wing of impossible longing,

I must fly, fly…

to my homeland, to see you) I shan't borrow the wing

of the sandgrouse[85] that's been tamed by the city.

I said: *I waited for you as sad clouds pass the heart's terraces to wash*

the fields of ash left by the mortars (I cast my shadow over the sea,

dividing it across the ships that sail towards Dilmun;[86]

the sea was disturbed by my words,

leaving the blue fragrance of my tears on the grass.

Spring is over while my heart is still a prisoner of the yellow leaves

swept by the wind to the edge of the garden)

I jump up from the earth's torment. I make a tablet of clay.

There will be no light more beautiful than the sun of freedom

the day we smash down the doors and summon tyrants to judgement;

(poets cluster stickily at festivals and I – depressed – stand up,

slam the door behind me,

head to an out-of-the-way pub).

Swatting away the buzzing of rhymes

and dreaming of the blue flowing under my eyelids

I walk alone on the sand in your footsteps

(but I can't reach…) the sea's waves are ferocious and rats

crunch my ship

while I wrestle the waves – O Lord –

there's no homeland in the ships.

I rise from the froth of the glass

and there's nothing there except soldiers and sand.

....

....

....

حاربتُ في جيشِ سرجون حتى أُسرتُ، ورابضتُ
خلف متاريس تشيلي حتى جُرحتُ،
وقاتلتُ في ثورةِ الزنجِ حتى قُتلتُ..
فما زادني الموتُ إلّا حياةً من السأمِ المرِّ، أعلُكُها في المقاهي
وتَعْلُكُني في المنافي...
وأصرخُ: ما كنتُ يا صاحبي شاهداً أخرساً فلماذا المُؤرّخُ
يحذفُ اسميَ؟... (ساعي البريدِ مضى بدموعي إلى اللهِ لكنّهُ
لمْ يعدْ... فمضيتُ إليكِ.

....

....

....

شفيفٌ كجنحِ الفَراشةِ قلبي، فكيفَ
سأزْفَأُهُ،
قلتُ أمضي إلى الغابِ.
هل في غصونكَ يا أثلُ من فسحةٍ
لطيوريَ
أتعبَها الأفقُ...
يلتفُّ نَحْلُ القصيدةِ
في شَعرِ مَنْ يعبرنَّ دمي،
يتطاوسنَ بين الزنودِ،
ووحدي أُحدّقُ في كتبي والمصابيح)

162

....

....

....

I fought in the army of Sarjoon until I was captured, and I placed myself
behind the fortifications of Chile, until I left;
I fought in the Zonj revolution until I was killed...

    so death gave me a life of bitter boredom to suck up in cafés,

      and chew me in exile.

I shout: *I was not a mute witness, my friend, so why did the historian*
scratch out my name?...(the postman took my tears to God but he never
returned...so I came to you).

....

....

....

    My heart is transparent as the wing of a butterfly, how can
I mend it?

    I said: *Let me go to the woods. O tamarisk,*

      is there a place in your branches

for my birds

which are tired by the endlessness of the horizon...?

A swarm of poems are buzzing round

    the hair of girls passing through my blood,

      flirtatious in someone's arms,

        (and me on my own staring at my books and lamps)

موحشةٌ روحُكَ. البحرُ ينأى...
وأنتَ ببطنِ السفينةِ
أقْصِدُ في جوفِ حوتِكَ
يا يونسُ العربيُّ
يَشُقُّ العبابَ
ويلقيكَ في جزرِ الواقِ واقِ،
وحيداً...

. . . .
. . . .
. . . .

– لماذا تركتَ بلادَكَ،
كانتْ لكَ الرطبَ – الخمرَ،
والجنّةَ البابليّةَ...
– لمْ أترِكِ الأرضَ من بطرٍ،
أيّها اللائمونَ بمقهى الشتاتِ،
ولكنّهُ الجمرُ لا يصطلي
غيرَ قابضِهِ...

...

سأرضى بما قَسَّمَ اللهُ لي في المنافي
سوى الذلِّ،
أطوي الدروبَ بأمعاءِ... فارغةٍ
وذهولٍ،
كأني
خرجتُ

164

your soul is gloomy. The sea goes far out...

but you are in the belly of the ship

or, verily, in the belly of your whale

O Arab Jonah;

it parts the waves

and casts you away on the Waq Waq Islands,

alone...

....

....

....

– Why did you leave your country?

The dates were yours – the wine

and the Babylonian heaven?

It wasn't that I was ungrateful,

O you that lay blame while lounging in cafés of exile,

but embers burn

whoever touches them.

...

I shall accept whatever God chooses for me in exile

except humiliation.

I cross the streets, empty inside,

bewildered

like

I just

من السجنِ
توّاً.
أعضُّ الحياةَ بأسنانِ روحي
وأصعدُ مزدهياً
بنشيدي
أخدّشُ وجةَ السماءِ لتُمْطِرَني...

كلُّ أرضٍ ستعشبُ فيها الأغاني بلادي...

أأرضى أُبدِّلُ أرضاً بأرضٍ؟
وكيفَ سأغفو،
وهذي الوسادةُ ليستْ ذراعيكِ
هذي الـ....

[صرختُ بهم:
البلادُ على ظهرِ حوتٍ.
فلا توقدوا قِدِرَ الحربِ...
لكنَّهم سخروا من ظنوني
فماجتْ بهم
قبلَ
أنْ
يلحقوا
بالمراكبِ...]

قلتُ: انتظرتُكَ...
نمضي معاً في الأزِقّةِ (لا بيتَ لي
غيرُ ظلِّ القصيدةِ

left

    prison

I bite on life with the teeth of my being

and rise up proud

      with my anthem

I scratch the sky to make it rain on me.

Wherever songs flourish will be my home.

If I exchange one land for another

how shall I sleep

    when this pillow is not your arms

    this is…

        (I warned them –

        This country's not dry land but the back of a whale;

        don't stoke war on it with your smouldering fires.

        They laughed in my face,

        and were shrugged

        off into

        the sea,

        out of reach

        of their ships).

I said: *I waited for you…*

to wander with you in the alleys (there's no home for me

      except the shade of a poem,

أفرشُهُ وأنامُ)

شريدين،

تُنكِرُنا واجهاتُ الفنادقِ

والطرقاتُ الغريبةُ

متكئاً فوق كَتفي،

يُبلِّلُ دمعُكَ عُشبَ قميصي

تُحَدِّثُني عن مسارِ الغيومِ بجفنيكَ

عن جوعِ طفليكَ في بلدِ النخلِ...

[كنتُ أراكَ وراءَ الزجاجِ المكيَّفِ عينين مثل الينابيعِ صافيتين،

وثغراً يبيساً كحقلِ بلادي، تُنَظِّفُ أرضِيَّةَ

البارِ (أعقابُهمْ والبصاقُ المخَتَّر فوق جروحي المندَّاةِ) تحني

أمامَ الموائدِ قامتَكَ – النخلَ (حيثُ إنْكَسَرتُ أمامَ السياطِ)

....

....

....

هل كانَ هذا الفراتُ

سوى دِمِنا المترقرقِ من عهدِ سُومَر

... حتى مصبِّ الحكوماتِ

تَكشِطُ عن جلدِنا الملحَ والانقلاباتِ...

نأتي ونمضي كما موجةٌ في فمِ البحرِ يزفُرُها...

لا نُخلِّفُ فوقَ السواحلِ غيرَ الزبدْ

كلُّ شيءٍ بدْ

وما نحنُ إلّا خيولُ سباقِ الأبدْ

which I throw to the ground like a mat to sleep on);

we are homeless,

hotels reject us

and strange roads

rest on my shoulders,

your tears wet my shirt

your eyelids tell me about the movement of clouds,

about the hunger of your two children in the land of palm trees.

I saw you behind the air-conditioned glass, two eyes like clear springs,

and a dry mouth like the fields of my country, cleaning the floor of the

bar (cigarette butts and thickened spit over my raw wounds) you stood

bowing over the food – the palm tree (where I was broken by the whip).

....

....

....

Is this Euphrates

nothing but our rippling blood from the age of Sumer?

...flowing into the pockets of governments

that flay us with salt and revolutions?

We come and go like waves in the mouth of the sea, breathed out...

nothing is created on our shores except foam.

All things dissipate

and we are nothing but horses on a race to eternity,

فلماذا وُلدنا، وفي عنقِنا حبلُ مشنقةٍ

تؤرجحُنا الريحُ ذاتَ المنافي...

وذاتَ البلدْ

1984–1996

وما بينهما من أيّام سود

السليمانية (إسطبل في قرية شيخ اوصال)، معسكر 575،

شيراتون البصرة، سجن الموقع في كركوك،

الكوفة، بغداد، القاهرة عمّان، صنعاء،

عدن، الخرطوم، دمشق،

بيروت

170

so why were we born with a hangman's rope round our necks

swinging in the wind between that exile…

and that land?

1984–1996

And in between

Suleimaniyah (a stable in the village of Shaikh Awsal),

Camp 575, Sheraton Al Basra, Prison in Kirkuk,

Al Kufa, Baghdad, Cairo, Amman, Sana'a,

Aden, Al Khartoum, Damascus,

Beirut.

عن عدنان الصائغ

ولد في مدينة الكوفة، العراق، عام 1955 ، وهو واحدٌ من أكثر الأصوات الأصيلة في جيل الشعراء العراقيين المعروف باسم حركة الثمانينيات.

يحمل شعره شغفاً شديداً بالحرية والحب والجمال. يستخدم عدنان كلماته كقوةٍ للتنديدِ بدمارِ الحرب وأهوال الديكتاتورية.

غادر وطنه عام 1993، وعاش في عمّان، ثمّ لجأ إلى بيروت، ثمّ إلى السويد عام 1996 ثمّ ليستقرّ منذ عام 2004 في منفاه بلندن.

عضوِ اتحاد الأدباء العراقيين، واتحاد الأدباء العرب، ونقابات الصحفيين العراقيين، والصحفيين العرب، ومنظمة الصحفيين العالمية، واتحاد الكتاب السويديين، ونادي القلم السويدي، والقلم الإنكليزي، وحبر الكتّاب المنفيين.

حصلَ على عدّةِ جوائز عالمية؛ من بينها جائزة هيلمان هاميت العالمية للشعر (نيويورك 1996)، وجائزة مهرجان الشِعر العالمي (روتردام 1997)، وجائزة اتحاد الكتاب السويديين (2005).

تمت دعوته لقراءة شعره في العديد من المهرجانات حول العالم.

نشر المجموعات الشِعرية التالية:

1. انتظريني تحت نصب الحُرّيَة – ط1 بغداد 1984.

2. أغنيات على جسر الكوفة – ط1 بغداد 1986، ط2 القاهرة 2011.

3. العصافير لا تحبُّ الرصاص – ط1 بغداد 1986.

4. سماء في خُوذَة – ط1 بغداد 1988، ط2 القاهرة 1991، ط3 القاهرة 1996.

5. مرايا لشَعرها الطويل – ط1 بغداد 1992، ط2 عَمّان – مدريد 2002، ط3 أوربرو السويد 2020.

About Adnan Al-Sayegh

Adnan Al-Sayegh, born in Al-Kufa in 1955, is one of the most original voices from the generation of Iraqi poets known as the Eighties Movement. His poetry carries an intense passion for freedom, love and beauty. Adnan uses his words as a weapon to denounce the devastation of war and the horrors of dictatorship. He left his homeland in 1993, lived in Amman and Beirut, then took refuge in Sweden in 1996. Since 2004 he has been living in exile in London.

Adnan is a member of the Iraqi and Arab Writers Unions, the Iraqi and Arab Journalists Unions, the International Journalist Organization, the Swedish Writers Union, the Swedish Pen Club, and English PEN and Exiled Writers Ink.

He has received several international awards, among them, the Hellman-Hammet International Poetry Award (New York 1996), the Rotterdam International Poetry Award (1997) and the Swedish Writers Association Award (2005), and has been invited to read his poems in many festivals across the world. The following collections of Adnan's poetry have been published:

1. *Wait for me under the Statue of Liberty* (Baghdad, 1984).
2. *Songs on the Bridge of Kufa* (Baghdad, 1986; Cairo, 2011).
3. *Sparrows Don't Love Bullets* (Baghdad, 1986).
4. *Sky in a Helmet* (Baghdad, 1988; Cairo 1991 and 1996).
5. *Mirrors for Her Long Hair* (Baghdad, 1992; Amman and Madrid, 2002; Örebro-Sweden, 2020).

6. غيمة الصمغ– ط1 بغداد 1993، ط2 دمشق 1994، ط3 القاهرة 2004.

7. تحت سماء غربية – ط1 لندن 1994، ط2 بيروت 2002، ط3 القاهرة 2006.

8. تكوينات – بيروت 1996.

9. نشيد أوروك "قصيدة طويلة" – ط1 بيروت 1996، ط2 بيروت 2006، ط3 بيروت – بغداد 2017(بـ 550 صفحة).

10. تأبَّط منْفى – ط1 السويد 2001، ط2 القاهرة 2006، ط3 بغداد 2015، ط4 البحرين – كندا 2017.

11. **و.. – ط1 بيروت 2011، ط2 بغداد 2015.**

وصدرت بعض أعماله الشعرية في ترجمات:

1. "مختارات شِعرية" (بالهولندية) ترجمة ياكو شونهوفن. (هولندا 1997).

2. "تحت سماء غربية" (بالاسبانية) ترجمة عبد الهادي سعدون، ومحسن الرملي. (اسبانيا، 1997).

3. "الكتابة بالأظافر" (بالسويدية) ترجمة ستافان ويسلاندر، والشاعرة بوديل جريك. (السويد 1998، 2000) .

4. "المحذوف من ..." مختارات شِعرية (بالإنكليزية) ترجمة الشاعر البريطاني ستيفن واتس، ومارغا برغي آرتاخو. (بريطانيا، 2009).

5. "تأبَّط منفى" (بالسويدية والعربية) ترجمة عدد من المترجمين، تحرير الشاعر السويدي آرنة زارنغ . (السويد، 2010).

6. "إنَّ القنابلَ لمْ تُفْطِرِ الآن" (بالإنكليزية والعربية) ترجمة د. عباس كاظم، وديفيد سليفان. (بريطانيا، 2013).

7. "الآن؛ كما قبلُ: ميزوبوتاميا– العراق" (بالانكليزية والعربية) بالاشتراك مع الشاعرة البريطانية جني لويس، (بريطانيا، مولفران برس، 2013).

8. غناءٌ لـ اينانا"؛ قصائد وأغنية (بالانكليزية والعربية) مع الشاعرة جني لويس، صاحبهما عزف على العود للفنانة باتريشا دي مايو . (بريطانيا، مولفران برس، 2014).

6. *Cloud of Glue* (Baghdad, 1993; Damascus, 1994; Cairo, 2004).

7. *Under a Strange Sky* (London, 1994; Beirut, 2002; Cairo, 2006).

8. *Formations* (Beirut, 1996).

9. *Uruk's Anthem* (Beirut, 1996, 2006 and 2017).

10. *Carrying his Exile under his Arm* (Sweden, 2001; Cairo, 2006; Baghdad, 2015; Bahrain and Canada, 2017).

11. *And* (Beirut, 2011; Baghdad, 2015).

And in translation –

1. *Poetry Selections* (Dutch), translated by Jaco Schoonhoven (Netherlands, 1997).

2. *Bajo Un Cielo Extranjero* (Spanish), translated by Abdul H. Sadoun and Muhisin Al-Ramly (Spain, 1997).

3. *Nagelskrift* (Swedish), translated by Bodil Greek and Staffan Wieslander (Sweden, 1998 and 2000).

4. *The Deleted Part* (English), translated by Stephen Watts and Marga Burgui-Artajo (United Kingdom, 2009).

5. *Att Bära Sin Exil* (Swedish & Arabic), translated by a number of translators, overseen by Arne Zaring (Sweden, 2010).

6. *Bombs Have Not Breakfasted Yet* (English), translated by Dr. Abbas Kadhim and David Sullivan (United Kingdom, 2013).

7. *Now as Then: Mesopotamia-Iraq*, poems in English and Arabic with the English poet, Jenny Lewis (UK, Mulfran Press, 2013).

8. *Singing for Inanna*, poems and a song in English and Arabic with the English poet Jenny Lewis and oud player Patricia de Mayo (United Kingdom, Mulfran Press, 2014).

9. "الشاعر الذي لا تصلُ رسائله إلى وطنه" مختارات شِعرية (بالفارسية). ترجمة سيد مهدي نژاد. (ايران ، 2014).

10. "القِمَّةُ بِئرٌ مَقْلوب" مختارات شعرية (بالفرنسية) ترجمة د. محمد صالح بن عمر . (فرنسا، 2015).

11. "أوراق من سيرة تأبَّط منفى" (بالإنكليزية والعربية) ترجمة ستيفن واتس، ومارغا برغي آرتاخو، (بريطانيا، دار آرك ، 2016).

12. "تأبط منفى" (بالانكليزية) ترجمة جواد وادي ومراجعة: ف. ك. فيليبس، و ج. نايت (بريطانيا، فالي برس، 2016).

13. "عشر قصائد" (بالإنكليزية والعربية) رسوم كيت هيزل، ترجمة: جني لويس، وعلاء جمعة (بريطانيا، مولفران برس، 2016).

14. "وليمة الغياب" (بالإسبانية) تحرير ومراجعة الشاعر إليا غالان، ترجمة: د. محسن الرملي، عبد الهادي سعدون، رول جيم كافيريا، روبرتو ماسكارو. (آرس بوتيكا، اسبانيا 2017).

15. عشر قصائد" (بالعربية والروسية والإنكليزية) رسوم كيت هيزل، الترجمة الروسية: ناتاليا دبروفينا. (بريطانيا، مولفران برس، 2018).

كما تمت ترجمة شعره أيضاً إلى الإيطالية، والرومانية، والكردية، والنرويجية، والألمانية، والدنماركية، واليابانية، والصينية، والهاواي.

9. *The poet whose letters do not reach his homeland* (Farsi), Selected Poems, translated by Mohammad Mehdi Nzad (Iran – Tehran, 2014).

10. *Le sommet est un puits* (French) *The top is an overturned well, Selected Poems*, translated by Dr. Mohamed Salah Ben Amor (France, 2015).

11. *Pages from the Biography of an Exile* (English) translated by Marga Burgui-Artajo and Stephen Watts (United Kingdom, Arc, 2016).

12. *To Cuddle My Exile* (English) translated by Jawad Wadi, edited by V. Q. Phillips and J. Knight (United Kingdom, Valley Press, 2016).

13. *Ten Poems,* short poems in English and Arabic, illustrated by Kate Hazell, translated by Jenny Lewis and Alaa Juma (United Kingdom, Mulfran Press, 2016).

14. *Banquete De Auisencias Extranjero* (Spanish), Editorial Director: Ilia Galán. Translated by Dr. Muhsin Al-Ramli, Abdul Hadi Sadoun, Raúl Jaime Gaviria and Roberto Mascaró (Spain, Ars Poetica, 2017).

15. *10 Cmuxo, Ten Poems*, in English, Russian and Arabic, illustrated by Kate Hazell, Russian translated by Natalya Dubrovina (United Kingdom, Mulfran Press, 2018).

His poetry has also been translated into Italian, Romanian, Kurdish, Norwegian, German, Danish, Japanese, Chinese and Hawaiian.

يقولُ عدنان:

– أنا انسانٌ حرٌّ تماماً. لا أرتبطُ بحزبٍ أو طائفةٍ أو قوميةٍ. لأني أومنُ أنَّ الأنسانَ هو مركزُ الكونِ، وهو أعلى قيمةٍ في الوجودِ، وبالتالي فهو أكبرُ من كلِّ هذه التقسيماتِ الجغرافيةِ أو المذهبيةِ. هو روحٌ حرَّةٌ ساميةٌ ذكيةٌ خلّاقةٌ، لا ينبغي لها أبداً أنْ تكونَ مقيَّدةً بشكلٍ ما.

التقاليدُ التي جئتُ منها مختلفة وملتبسة تماماً، لذا جعلتُ من الفكرِ الإنسانيِّ الحرِّ، ومن الفنِّ الشعريِّ، مرجعاً ومرتكزاً وطريقاً...

هل الحربُ حتمية؟ عندما يتعلَّمُ الإنسانُ ويسمو، فلنْ يُفكرَ بالاقتتالِ، بل بالحوارِ والسلامِ والتعاونِ المثمرِ لبناءِ حياةٍ أفضلَ...

الحروبُ لغةُ الأقوامِ البدائيةِ عندما كان فكرُهم غيرَ قادرٍ على التحاورِ مع الآخرِ أو استيعابِهِ...

لذا فالثقافةُ هي صمَّامُ أمانٍ للبشريةِ.

مقتبس من مقابلة أجرتها معه كوليت شيريدان
في مهرجان كورك الأدبي، الذي عُقد في ايرلندا
الخميس، 23 نوفمبر 2017.

Adnan says

– 'I am a completely free man, not associated with a party, religion or nationality. I believe that humans are the centre of the universe and have the highest value in existence. Therefore, they are greater than geographical or sectarian divisions. They are creative souls who should never be constrained in any way. The traditions from which I come are very different and ambiguous, so I have made out of the human's free thought and poetic art, a reference, base and path.

Are wars inevitable? When people learn and grow, they will not think of fighting, but of dialogue, peace and fruitful co-operation to build a better life. Wars are the language of primitive people who are unable to interact with or assimilate their thoughts. Therefore, knowledge is a safety valve for humanity.'

Adapted from an interview with Colette Sheridan
for the Cork Literary Festival, The Irish Examiner
Thursday 23 November, 2017.

عن المترجمين

جني لويس؛ استاذة الشِعر في جامعة أكسفورد، وهي شاعرة وكاتبة مسرحياتٍ وأغانٍ ومترجمة.

قدمت ثمانية أعمال مسرحية ودورات شعرية في المسارح الرئيسية بما في ذلك مسرح ليستر هيماركت، ومسرح البولكا (للأطفال)، والقاعة الملكية للاحتفالات، ومسرح بيغاسوس في أكسفورد حيث عملت هناكَ مدرسةً للكتابة الأساسية لمدة 20 عاماً.

كما صدر لها أيضاً أربع مجاميع شعرية: "عندما أصبحتُ أمازونية " (عن دار آيرون للنشر، 1996)، "القامة" (شعراء أكسفورد/ دار كاركانيت 2007)، "أخُذُ بلادٍ ما بين النهرين" (شعراء أكسفورد/ كاركانيت 2014)، "إعادة روي گلگامش" (كاركانيت 2018)، كما نشرت جني كتابين صغيرين باللغة الإنجليزية والعربية بالاشتراك مع عدنان الصائغ: "الآنَ كما قبلُ: ميزوبوتاميا – العراق" (دار (مولفران للنشر - 2013)، و"غناءٌ لـ اينانا" (مولفران 2014)؛ كجزءٍ من مشروع "كتابة بلاد ما بين النهرين" الحائز على تقدير مجلس الفنون والذي يهدف إلى بناء الجسور وتعزيز الصداقات بين المجتمعات الناطقة باللغتين الإنجليزية والعربية.

كان "إعادة كتابة گلگامش" كتاب الدولة الجديد للسنة، وكاركنت كتاب العام ومراجعة لندن للكتب "كتاب الأسبوع" عند النشر. وحالياً تكمل جني دراستها في الدكتوراه عن جلجامش في كلية گولدسميث، جامعة لندن.

About the Translators

Jenny Lewis is a poet, playwright, translator and songwriter who teaches poetry at Oxford University. She has had eight plays and poetry cycles performed at major theatres including the Leicester Haymarket, The Polka Theatre (for children), the Royal Festival Hall and Pegasus Theatre, Oxford where she was a Core Writing Tutor for 20 years. She has also published four full collections of poetry – *When I Became an Amazon* (Iron Press, 1996), *Fathom* and *Taking Mesopotamia* (Oxford Poets/Carcanet, 2007/2014), *Gilgamesh Retold* (Carcanet Press, 2018) – and two chapbooks in English and Arabic with Adnan Al-Sayegh, *Now as Then: Mesopotamia-Iraq* and *Singing for Inanna* (Mulfran Press, 2013/2014) as part of the award-winning, Arts Council-funded 'Writing Mesopotamia' project which aims to build bridges and foster friendships between English and Arabic-speaking communities. *Gilgamesh Retold* was a *New Statesman* Book of the Year, a Carcanet Book of the Year and a *London Review of Books* Bookshop 'Book of the Week' on publication. She is currently completing a PhD on Gilgamesh at Goldsmiths, London University.

ربى أبو غيدا؛ شاعرة ومؤلفة. قامت بنشر مجموعة شعرية بعنوان "دروب ودهاليز" باللغة العربية والتي تُرجمت إلى اللغة الإنجليزية (صدرت عن دار نشر ألبيون بيتنيك عام 2019). فازت قصتها القصيرة "رياح سيروكو" بالجائزة الأولى في رايترز أند أرتيستس يربوك عام 2014.

تترجم الشعر ورواية الخيال باللغتين العربية والإنجليزية.

حصلت على درجة الكتابة الإبداعية من جامعة أكسفورد، وماجستير دراسات في الكتابة الإبداعية من جامعة كامبريدج. وهي الآن تكمل درجة الماجستير في SOAS، جامعة لندن.

نُشرتْ كتاباتها، بما في ذلك القصص القصيرة والشعر والمراجعات، في العديد من المنشورات في المملكة المتحدة وأمريكا الشمالية ولبنان.

Ruba Abughaida is a poet and author. She has published a collection of poetry called *Paths and Passageways* in Arabic which was translated into English (published by Albion Beatnik Press in 2019). Her short story 'The Sirocco Winds' won first prize in the Writers and Artists Historical Fiction competition in 2014. She translates poetry and fiction in Arabic and English. She holds a creative writing degree from Oxford University and an Master of Studies in creative writing from Cambridge University. She is currently completing an Master of Studies at SOAS, London University. Her writing, including short stories, poetry and reviews, has appeared in several publications in the UK, North America and Lebanon.

ملاحظات عن الترجمة

- ## جني لويس:

عملنا عدنان وأنا منذ 2012 على ترجمةِ أعماله إلى الإنجليزية وأعمالي إلى العربية. وقد تمَّ الارتقاء بنهج العمل في 2013 بأفضل التعزيزات بعد حصولنا على أولِ منحةٍ من مجلس الفنون،

وعندها تمكَّنا أنْ نعملَ مع ربى أبوغيدا؛ كاتبة فلسطينية لبنانية، سبقَ لي أنْ درَّستها في جامعة أكسفورد. كما أنها ناطقة باللغتين بطلاقة وحائزة على جائزة بالكتابة الروائية، ربى شاعرةٍ ذاتَ موهبةٍ، سريعةَ التأقلم ولها حاسةٌ ثاقبةٌ للنصِّ. وهذا يكون مثالياً، للذهاب إلى شعرِ عدنان ذي التأويلاتِ والمتعدِّدِ النواحي.

بعد أنْ زوَّدتنا ربى بالمسودةِ الأولى من ترجمتها للنصِّ، بقينا عدنان وأنا، منكبَّين، ما بلغَ مئاتِ الساعات خلال الأعوام السبعة الماضية في قراءاتٍ وتفسيراتٍ مكثفةٍ مقرَّبةٍ، نستطلعُ جوانبَ كلِّ سطرٍ ومقطعٍ لكي نستخرجَ أكبر قدرٍ ممكنٍ من "عصارته".

لمراتٍ عديدة كانت تستوقفُنا صورةٌ أو طريقةُ تعبيرٍ خلال مساراتنا. ماذا كان المغزى الحقيقي؟

في أوقاتٍ كان يصعبُ حتى على عدنان أن يُوضِّحَ – خصوصا في التعامل مع المجاز، الرمزية، السريالية، الفكاهة المحلية، أو وقائع حلم وهذيان.

كيف نلتقطُ بلغةٍ وثقافةٍ أخرى شيئاً سريعَ الزوال، كما تراءى لـ فرجينيا وولف في مذكراتها اليومية مثل ومضة، زعنفة، في محيط الرؤية، وذلك هو جوهر الإبداع.

عندما يقرأُ عدنان بصوتٍ عالٍ من نشيد أوروك، فأنَّ التغني المقفى وإيقاعاتِ الصوتِ العربي يبدو وكأنه موسيقى، متعددة

Notes on Translation:

• **Jenny Lewis**

Adnan and I have been working on translations of his work into English
and my work into Arabic since 2012. The process was greatly enhanced
when, in 2013, after being awarded our first Arts Council grant, we were
able to work with Ruba Abughaida, a Palestinian-Lebanese writer whom
I had previously taught at Oxford. As well as being fluently bi-lingual
and an award-winning fiction writer, Ruba is a gifted poet with a
quickness of perception and acute sensitivity to text that is ideal when
applied to Adnan's mercurial, multifaceted poetry. After Ruba had
supplied us with the first draft of a translation, Adnan and I then spent
what has amounted to hundreds of hours over the past seven years on
intense close reading and interpretation, interrogating every aspect of
each line and verse to extract as much 'juice' as we possibly could.
Several times an image or idiom would stop us in our tracks. What was
the real meaning? Sometimes it was hard for even Adnan to explain –
especially when dealing with metaphor, symbolism, surrealism, local
humour or episodes of dreaming and delirium. How do you capture in
another language and culture something as evanescent as what Virginia
Woolf, in a diary entry, saw as a flicker, a fin on the periphery of vision,
that is the essence of creativity?

When Adnan reads aloud from *Uruk's Anthem* the singing
rhymes and rhythms of the original Arabic sound like music; an extended

النغمات وممتدة، تبهجُ حتى

جمهوراً ناطقاً بالإنجليزية ولا يفهم اللغة.

بدلاً من محاولة اعادة المتماثل شكليا للميزاتِ الصوتية، أردتُ أنْ

ألتقطَ روحَ القصيدة، ورؤيتها في قالب موسيقي قريب، ربما من "تحت غابة الحليب"

لديلان توماس أو المتابعة العادلة لجون برنسايد – كلاهما انتدبا للراديو.

لقد عملتُ ذلك بقدرِ الخطى كأي شيء آخر، رغم امتداد الأسطرِ والتلاعبِ بالوقفاتِ،

كونهما مهمان جدا في الشعر باللغة الإنكليزية، يتم استعمالهما هنا بحريةٍ تامةٍ لدعم

محتوى ومعنى النص

بشكلٍ كاملٍ.

مع تأتّي عدنان لاختيارِ نصوص من هذا الكتاب حاول أنْ يعطي فكرةً

عن التوجهِ السرديِّ الكامن للمفهومِ بأكملهِ بحيث تتواتر المراجعُ والوقائعُ (المدونات)

وأحياناً مع تبدُّلاتٍ في الثيمةِ.

بعضُ السماتِ في النصِّ العربي، مثلاً الفاصلة والسخرية وخلط صيغ الأفعال، تكونُ

غريبةً إلى حد ما في الشعرِ المعاصرِ باللغة الإنجليزية

ولكنها عنصرٌ مقبولٌ (حتى وإنْ كانَ ساخراً أحياناً) في الشعرِ

العربيِّ وتمَّ الاحتفاظ به.

عناصر أخرى، كالأقواسِ غير المغلقة والنقاط الزاخرة الممتدة، وهذا الشيء المميَّزُ في

أسلوبِ عدنان والمقصود منه الدلالة على الهذيانِ والفوضى،

وقد تم نشره، في الأقل، في هذا الظهور الرئيسي ولأول مرة في عالم الشعر الناطق باللغة

الانجليزية.

عند نهاية عملنا سويةً لهذا الكتاب، عدنان وأنا، نظرنا إلى جذرِ الكلمات، ومن

أين تحدَّرت. وكنتُ أطبّقُ منهجَ هيني في شعري وأحاول أنْ أستخدمَ الكلماتِ الأنجلو

ساكسونية حيثما أمكنَ ذلك، علماً أنَّ صلابتها ستضيفُ

polyphony which delights even English-speaking audiences who can't understand the language. Rather than attempt to replicate these sonic qualities formally, I wanted to try to capture the spirit of the poem, seeing it, in musical terms, a close relative, perhaps, of Dylan Thomas's *Under Milk Wood* or John Burnside's *The Fair Chase* – both commissioned for the radio. I have done this as much with pace as anything, although line lengths and the manipulation of hiatus, so important in English language poetry, are here deployed more loosely, to support the content and meaning of the text as a whole.

With the careful selections Adnan has chosen for this book he has tried to give an idea of the underlying narrative thrust of the whole concept in which characters, references and incidents (notes) recur, like variations on a theme. Some traits in the Arabic text, for example apostrophe, bathos and the mixing of tenses, are somewhat alien to contemporary English language poetry but an accepted ingredient (sometimes ironic) of Arab poetry and have been kept in. Other elements, such as unclosed brackets and copious, extended ellipses, which are idiosyncratic to Adnan's own practice and intended to denote incoherence and derangement, have been left out, at least for this first, major debut into the world of English-speaking poetry.

Towards the end of our work together on this book, Adnan and I have been looking at etymology, where words come from, as places of origin imbue them with as many different flavours as the people who speak them. I apply Heaney's own methodology to my own poetry and try to use Anglo Saxon words where possible, knowing that their sturdiness will add

صدقاً لشعري.

طبقتُ ذلك في ترجمتي لأعمال عدنان. وماذا أيضاً؟

بفضل ليرنارد أودونوهيو، مشرفي على القصائد الغنائية في أوكسفورد عندما درستُ هناك كطالبةٍ مُطّلِعةٍ، كان اهتمامي ومعرفتي بشعرِ التروبادرو والحضارةِ الموريةِ الأندلسيةِ التي أنشأته، وهذا ساعدني إلى حدٍّ كبيرٍ في فهمِ جوانبٍ من شعرِ عدنان.

أحببتُ دائماً اطروحةَ ابن حزم في العشق، طوق الحمامة، التي كتبها في سنة 1022. وقد اُكتشفَ مؤخراً أنَّ ذلك الحَمامَ في ذاك الوقت كان له أطواقٌ حول الأعناقِ مصنوعةٌ من مادةٍ مغناطيسيةٍ تساعدُ الحمامةَ على ايجاد طريقِها إلى البيت.

أرى أنَّ هذا مجازٌ مناسبٌ لكيفيةِ العثورِ على طريقِ العودةِ إلى البيتِ كالشاعرِ أو المترجِمِ على حدٍّ سواء.

جيني لويس،

نيسان 2020.

- **ربى أبو غيدا**

اعتبرتُهُ حظاً سعيداً عندما وطأتْ قدماي صفَّ جني لويس في جامعةِ أكسفورد قبلَ سنواتٍ قليلةٍ. كان تركيزي أنْ أختتمَ روايتي من خلال دراستي للكتابةِ الإبداعيةِ رغمَ استمتاعي بقراءةِ الشعر حيثُ لمْ يكنْ نمط كتابةٍ فكرتُ به.

كلُّ هذا تغيّرَ خلالَ أسابيع. أصبحتُ أسبرُ أغوارَ الشعرِ نتيجةَ التشجيعِ الهادفِ من جني.

خلال انشغالي بالدراسةِ، حدَّثتني عن شاعرٍ عراقيٍّ التقتْ به في أمسيةٍ شعريةٍ. طلبتْ مني فيما بعد أنْ أترجمَ شعرَها وكذلك شعرَهُ.

تردَّدتُ في باديءِ الأمرِ. أليستِ الترجمةُ مناطةً بمترجمين معتمدين وخبراء باللغةِ؟ على أيِّ حالٍ قبلتُ.

عندما أتذكّرُ ما انتابني من أحاسيس وقد بدثْ ضاغطة.

honesty to my own poetry. This I have applied to my translation of Adnan's work. And what else? Thanks to Bernard O'Donoghue, my supervisor on Lyric Poetry at Oxford when I studied there as a mature student, my interest in, and knowledge of, troubadour poetry and the Moorish-Andalusian culture it grew out of have helped me greatly in my understanding of parts of Adnan's poetry. I have always loved Ibn' Hazm's treatise on love, *The Dove's Neck Ring*, written in 1022. It has been recently discovered that doves of that era did have a ring round their necks made of a magnetic material which would help the dove find its way home. I see this as an appropriate metaphor of how to find one's way home. Both as a poet and a translator.

Jenny Lewis,

April, 2020.

• **Ruba Abughaida**

I consider it my good fortune to have walked into Jenny Lewis' class some years ago at Oxford University. I was focused on finishing a novel as part of my creative writing degree and although I enjoyed reading poetry, it wasn't a writing platform I had considered. All of that changed within a few weeks. Jenny's gentle encouragement tipped me into its waters where I waded with enthusiasm. As the course progressed, she spoke to me about an Iraqi poet she had met at a reading. She asked if I would translate some poetry of hers, then of his. I was hesitant. Wasn't that reserved for professional translators and language experts? I said yes anyway. Looking back I can still feel how overwhelming it seemed.

لَمْ تتكوَّنْ لدي خارطةُ طريقٍ لترجمةِ شعرِ جني وعدنان إلى لغةٍ أخرى ممزوجةٍ بجمالِ وفسحةِ شِعرِهِما.

مع مرورِ الشهورِ أثناءَ العملِ معهما تعزَّزتْ لدي رؤيةٌ لما هو مستطاعٌ وضروريٌّ للترجمةِ.

أدركتُ مكانةَ شعرِ عدنان في موقعِ الشِعرِ العراقي المعاصر. استمتعتُ بباقة تركيبة شِعرِ جني الذي يغرسُ بطريقةٍ قويةٍ وانسيابيةٍ.

دفعني عمقُ نشيد أروك وحجمُهُ إلى تحدي تصوراتي حول أفضلِ طريقةٍ للترجمة. كان المطلوبُ أنْ أضعَ على حدةٍ كل ما ظننتُ أني أعرفُهُ لأترك الصفحاتِ تتنفسُ في لغةٍ ثانيةٍ.

قفزتِ الكلماتُ من الصفحةِ طالبةً الحضورَ. وكانتْ هناكَ معانٍ تظهرُ بعد أيامٍ وأنا أشربُ كوباً من شاي زنجبيل أو أشاهدُ العصافيرَ تسترخي على الأشجارِ بمحاذاة نافذتي.

العملُ ذو شرائح مع فورةٍ تجيءُ نتيجة تجربةِ حربٍ وتشرُّدٍ.

الصوتُ يقظٌ، واضحٌ، محتارٌ، متسائلٌ، ساخرٌ، ساخطٌ.

تعلَّقتُ بإحساسِها بسرعةٍ ووجدتُ أنَّ تلكَ القصائدَ قد التصقتْ بي فترةً طويلةً بعدَ ترجمةِ أخرِ كلمةٍ.

وما زالتِ التجربةُ باقيةً معي.

إثباتاً لحرفية جني وعدنان كشاعرين استطاعا إيجادَ لغةٍ مشتركةٍ بينهما: لغة ثالثة صامتة ازدهرتْ وأظهرتْ نفسَها بشكلٍ شعريٍّ.

عندما تعرفت عليهما بدا لي أنَّ صداقتهما قد تواصلتْ لسنواتٍ مديدةٍ.

يتحادثان بإلمامِ كتّابٍ يدركون الجانبَ المعرفيَّ الآخرَ فيما بينهما.

أصبحَ واضحاً لي عندَ تبادلِ المسوَّداتِ أنهما مُتعمِّقانِ بحرفةٍ صنعتهما وأنهما قارئين نهمين.

يحبانِ التاريخ مثلي

I had no clear idea of how to portray the beauty and expansiveness of Jenny and Adnan's poems in another language. But as the months passed, working with them enhanced my view of what is possible and what is necessary when translating. I understood the importance of Adnan's work to the contemporary Iraqi poetry scene. I revelled in the variety of poetic structures that powerfully and gracefully infuse Jenny's work.

The depth and scale of *Uruk's Anthem* challenged my perceptions of how best to translate. I had to put aside what I thought I knew and let the pages breathe in a different language. The words leapt out of the page demanding an audience. There were meanings that would appear days later as I drank a cup of ginger tea or watched the birds settle in the trees outside my window. The work is layered with an intensity that comes out of the experience of war and displacement. The voice is alert, clear, puzzled, questioning, ironic, wry. I related to its sense of urgency and found that the poems clung to me long after the last word had been translated. The experience remains with me still.

It is a testament to the calibre of poets that Jenny and Adnan are that they were able to find another common language between them: a third silent language that thrived and revealed itself in poetic form. When I met them it seemed as though they had a friendship that spanned a lifetime. They communicate with the familiarity of writers who recognise the other-worldly aspect in each other. It became apparent to me as we exchanged drafts how intricately they knew their craft and that they were extremely well read. They like history, as I do, and their

وشِعرُهما يمنح القرَّاءَ مساحةً جديدةً لاستكشافِ التخيلاتِ.
ولهما قدرةٌ فريدةٌ لكتابةِ أقدمِ المروياتِ والمؤثراتِ
بطريقةٍ حديثةٍ ومثيرةٍ.
التعاونُ معهما هو واحدٌ من المسرَّاتِ الإبداعيةِ خلالَ رحلتي كشاعرةٍ.
كثيرا ما أعودُ لأعمالهما المفردةِ من أجلِ الإلهامِ والمتعةِ.

ربى أبو غيداء،
نيسان 2020.

poetry gives readers new territories to explore through their imagination. They have the rare ability to write the most ancient of stories and emotions in a new and exciting way. Collaborating with them is one of the many creative delights along my journey as a poet. I often go back to their individual work for inspiration and for pleasure.

Ruba Abughaida,

April, 2020.

آراء في النتاج الشعري لعدنان الصائغ

عدنان الصائغ، شاعرٌ مبدعٌ يواصلُ مسيرته عبر حرائقِ الشِعرِ ويغمسُ كلماته بدم القلب. يرحلُ عبر الجزئياتِ الصغيرة للحياةِ العراقيةِ في صيرورتها، بكلماتٍ واضحةٍ بسيطةٍ، مثقلةٍ بالبذورِ والزهورِ والثمار.

عبد الوهاب البياتي (1926–1999)،

من رُوّاد الشِعر العربي الحديث.

إذا ما عُرِف الإيطاليون بالأوبرا، والفرنسيون بالفنِ التشكيليِّ، والإنكليزُ بالمسرح، فإنَّ العراقيين إنَّما عُرِفوا بالشِعرِ منذُ گلگامش أقدم ملحمةٍ شعريةٍ في العالم. إنَّهم يتنفَّسون، أو يعبِّرون عن أنفسِهم شِعراً. وأنْ تُوجِدَ لكَ اسماً من بين آلافِ الأسماءِ الشعريةِ، كما فعلَ عدنان الصائغ عن جدارةٍ، فذلكَ إنجازٌ ليس بالهيِّن. عدنان الصائغ يتمتعُ بصوتِه الخاصِّ، وهو فنانٌ يثيرُ الإعجابَ وعلى درجةٍ عاليةٍ.

د. صلاح نيازي،

شاعر، ومترجم رواية "يوليسس" لـ جيمس جويس.

عدنان الصائغ شاعرٌ تنتبهُ إلى صوتِه حالما تسمعهُ بين مئاتِ الأصواتِ اللاغطةِ بالشِعر. فالشِعرُ اليوم كثيرٌ جداً، ولكنْ ما يستحقُّ أنْ يُصغى إليه قليل جداً. وشِعر عدنان الصائغ من هذا القليل.

جبرا إبراهيم جبرا (1920–1994)،

كاتب وناقد أكمل دراسته في القدس،

ثمَّ في جامعة كامبريدج.

Reviews of Adnan Al-Sayegh's work

Adnan Al-Sayegh is a creative poet pursuing his path through the fires of poetry...He migrates through the little details of Iraqi life, in its very essence, with simple, clear, and fruitful words.

Abdul-Wahab Al-Bayati (1926–1999),
one of the modern pioneers of Arabic poetry.

If the Italians are known for their operas, the French for their paintings, and the English for their dramas, the Iraqis, since the oldest epic in the world is Gilgamesh, are known for their poetry. People there breathe poetry, and to make a name for yourself among the huge host of names as Adnan Al-Sayegh has deservedly done, is no small achievement. Al-Sayegh has his own voice, and is an admirable craftsman of high calibre.

Dr. Salah Niazi,
Poet and translator of James Joyce's Ulysses into Arabic.

Adnan Al-Sayegh is a poet whose voice attracts your attention when you hear him among the hundreds of other voices that rant with poetry. For poetry is abundant nowadays. However, very little is worthy of being listened to. Adnan's poetry is part of this worthy little.

Jabra Ibrahim Jabra (1920–1994),
a writer and critic who was educated
in Jerusalem and, later, at Cambridge.

من المؤكدِ أنْ يشتملَ شعرُ الصائغ على تجاربِهِ الذاتيةِ، في القهرِ والحربِ والمنفى. على أنَّ لشعرِهِ صدىً قوياً يتجاوزُ حدودَ الجانبِ الشخصي.

غلين بورسغلوف،

مجلة آكيومن، آيار 2017 – العدد 88.

يقولُ عدنان الصائغ في قصيدتِهِ "يوليسيس": "كيفَ تغدو المنافي سجوناً بلا أسيجة". هذا الضغطُ – الناجمُ عن الرغبةِ في استشعارِ الأمانِ، والإحساسِ بالمرارةِ والألمِ، بسببِ فقدانِ منزلِك وعائلتِك وأصدقائِك – هو القوةُ الدافعةُ وراءَ شعرِهِ الاستثنائي.

إيان هاركر،

مجلة الشمال، يناير 2017 – العدد 57.

عن "أوراق من سيرة تأبط منفى"

"أوراقٌ من سيرة منفى"؛ هي مجموعة مشحونة بالسياسةِ، ضاربةٌ بقوةٍ، ومثيرةٌ للتفكيرِ، كتبها أحدُ أشهر الشعراء العراقيين "عدنان الصائغ". يبحرُ بنا من خلالِ مجموعتِهِ تلكَ، النضالِ المُضني فيما لاق بعد إجبارِهِ على النفي. إنَّهُ مرهفٌ، صريحٌ، ومؤثرٌ إلى حدٍّ بعيدٍ... بلا شكٍّ إنَّ هذا النتاجَ الضخمَ لهذا الشاعرِ الرائع هو "نشيد أوروك" المؤلف من 550 صفحة، والذي نُشر في بيروت عام 1996... لا يزالُ نصُّهُ الكاملُ ينتظرُ الترجمةَ، إلّا إنَّهُ يمكنُ للمرءِ أنْ يستشعرَ بطبيعةِ الحياةِ الواضحةِ المتواصلةِ في عالمِ المدنِ التي مزَّقتها الحروب.

إيان برينتون،

مجلة "Tears in the Fence" – 2016.

Al-Sayegh's poetry is, naturally, informed by his own experiences of persecution, war and exile, but this is poetry with powerful resonances that go far beyond the merely personal.

Glyn Pursglove,

Acumen, May 2017, No. 88.

'All exile now', says Adnan Al-Sayegh in his poem 'Ulysses', 'is a prison without walls.' This tension – the relief at having found safety and the grief and pain at the loss of your home, your family and your friends – is the driving force behind his extraordinary poetry.

Ian Harker,

The North, January 2017, No. 57.

On *Pages from the Biography of an Exile*

[*Pages from the Biography of an Exile* is a] politically charged, hard-hitting and thought-provoking collection by one of Iraq's best-known poets, Adnan Al-Sayegh. Throughout this collection, Adnan explores the exhausting struggle for acceptance after being forced into exile. Passionate, outspoken and incredibly moving...the *magnum opus* of this remarkable poet is surely the 550-page *Uruk's Anthem*, published in Beirut in 1996...the main body of which still awaits translation, but one can feel the palpable nature of life enduring within a world of war-torn cities.

Ian Brinton,

Tears in the Fence, 2016.

"أوراقٌ من سيرةٍ منفى"؛ أحدثُ مجموعةٍ شعريةٍ مترجمةٍ، كتبها أحدُ الشعراءِ العراقيين البارزين على نطاقٍ واسع. يأخذ عدنان الصائغ قرّاءةُ في رحلةٍ عاصفةٍ. هي مزيجٌ من العنفِ والمقاومةِ والنفيِّ السياسيّ. إذ إنّ الشعرَ يرافقُ الصائغ منذُ أيامِهِ كجنديٍّ في الحربِ العراقيةِ-الإيرانيةِ. فتجربتُهُ تتحدّثُ عالياً بقوةِ الحقائقِ؛ نفيه إلى الأردنِ، ولبنان، والسويد، وفي نهايةِ المطافِ إلى المملكةِ المتحدةِ، لتتبعَها معاناةُ الاندماجِ وتقبُّلِ غربته، وهي عواملٌ وضعتهُ في المواجهةِ.

من 15 مجموعة شعرية جديدة للقراءة خلال
شهر الشعر الوطني. *E.C Miller, Bustle 2017.*

من "10 قصائد"

(الشعراءُ الأقصرُ قامة/ كثيراً ما يضعونَ لقصائدِهم/ كعوباً عالية) بالرغم من صغرِ حجمِها، فإنّها عشرةُ قصائد تستحقُّ الثناء. إنّ للنصوصِ القصيرةِ للصائغِ القدرة لأنْ تمتاز بالبراعةِ والعذوبةِ: (عندما لمْ بزْني البحرُ/ ترك لي عنوانَهُ/ زرقةً عيميكِ/ وغادرني). كما أنّها لمَّحَتْ بضرباتٍ متقنةٍ إلى مواطنِ الغرورِ والجشعِ (منطرحاً/ على السفحِ/ يسألُ/ هل من شاغرٍ/ في القمّةِ؟). لمْ أكنْ لأتوقعْ أنّ هذه السطورَ السائرةَ بثقةٍ هي عبارةٌ عن نصٍّ مُترجَم.

أليسون براكينبوري،
"مراجعات *PN" 2017.*

198

Pages from the Biography of an Exile is the latest translated collection by one of Iraq's most widely recognised poets. Adnan Al–Sayegh takes readers through a tumultuous journey of violence, resistance, and political exile, as the poetry follows Al–Sayegh from his days as a conscript in the Iran-Iraq war; his experience speaking hard truths to power; his exile to Jordan, Lebanon, Sweden, and ultimately the United Kingdom; and the struggles of assimilation and acceptance his exile forced him to face.

15 New Poetry Collections To Read During
National Poetry Month, E.C Miller, Bustle, 2017.

Of *Ten Poems*

'Short poets / often put high heels / on their poems.' Though pocket-sized, *Ten Poems* deserves the highest praise. Al–Sayegh's tiny works can be witty and tender: 'The sea came when I was out. / It left me its address in the blue of your eyes.' They also aim precise blows at vanity and greed. 'Lounging / at the foot of the mountain / he asks / "Is there a vacancy at the top?"' I would not have guessed that these confidently paced lines were translations.

Alison Brackenbury,
PN Review, 2017.

عن "إنَّ القنابلَ لمْ تفطِرِ الآنَ" – ترجمة د. عباس كاظم وديفيد سليڤان، المملكة المتحدة – 2013

مثل العديد من الشعراءِ الموهوبين من جيلِه، أولئكَ الذين نشأوا في زمنِ الحرب. اضطرَّ عدنان الصائغ إلى ارتداءِ قناعِ الجنديِّ، والوقوف ضدَّ إرادتِهِ، على الحدودِ الشرقيةِ للعراق، لخوضِ حربٍ ضدَّ أخرين.

لقد كتبَ عدنان الصائغ معظمَ قصائدِهِ في الخفاءِ، بينما هو قابعٌ في قلبِ الحُفَرِ والخنادقِ التي امتدَّت على طولِ الأرضِ الحرامِ بين العراق وإيران، لينشرَها بعد سنواتٍ عقبَ وصولِهِ إلى منفاهُ الآمن. فقد تمَّ جمعُ العديدِ من قصائدِهِ الأخرى بمجردِ خروجِهِ من العراق، لترتقي بالصائغِ إلى مصافِ أحدِ أهمِ الشعراءِ العراقيين الموجودين على قيدِ الحياةِ اليوم.

د. عباس كاظم،

كاليفورنيا – 2013.

عن "مقتطفات من نشيد أوروك" – "مجلة "القصيدة الطويلة" العدد 15 – 2016

التقيتُ عدنان الصائغ لأولِ مرَّةٍ عام 2010 في أمسيةٍ للشعرِ الحديثِ عن الترجمةِ، عندما كنتُ محررةً مشاركةً في مجلة "القصيدة الطويلة" إذ دعوتُهُ لأنْ يرسلَ لنا مساهمتَهُ. وسُرعان ما اكتشفتُ (من خلالِ الترجمةِ) أنَّ نصاعةَ قصائدِهِ وصدقَها، تمتزجُ بشكلٍ لا يُنسى مع موسيقى صوتِهِ المتأصِّل. بعد مرورِ عَقدٍ على تلكَ الجلسةِ الأولى، ومع إضافةِ كتبِهِ ومنشوراتِهِ إلى رفوفي، فإنَّهُ لأمرٌ مُلهِمٌ أنْ يصلَ أخيراً شِعرُ عدنان الصائغ ذو الطرازِ العالميِّ إلى جمهورٍ أوسع من الناطقين باللغةِ الإنكليزيةِ في العالمِ. وعملُ جني لويس جزءٌ لا يتجزَّأُ من هذهِ العمليةِ، وتلكَ شهادةٌ على هذا التعاونِ الثريِّ والمُجزي.

لوسي هاميلتون،

كامبريدج.

Introduction to *Bombs Have Not Breakfasted Yet* (English), translated by Dr. Abbas Kadhim and David Sullivan (United Kingdom, 2013)

Like many talented poets of his generation, those who matured in wartime, Adnan Al-Sayegh had to wear the mask of a warrior and stand against his will at the eastern border of Iraq to fight someone else's war. In the foxholes and the trenches that spanned the no-man's land between Iraq and Iran, he wrote most of his secret poems that were published years later when he reached the safety of exile. Once he was out of Iraq, many other poems were added to make Al-Sayegh one of the most important Iraqi poets alive today.

Dr. Abbas Kadhim,
California, 2013.

Of *Extracts from Uruk's Anthem, Long Poem Magazine*, 15, 2016

I first met Adnan Al-Sayegh in 2010 at a Modern Poetry in Translation event when, as a co-editor of Long Poem Magazine, I invited him to send us a contribution. I soon discovered that the clarity and integrity of his poems (in translation), combine unforgettably with the music of his native voice. A decade on since that first meeting, and with his pamphlets and books added to my shelves, it's inspiring that Adnan Al-Sayegh's world-class poetry is at last reaching a wider audience in the English-speaking world; and that Jenny Lewis's own work is integral to that process is testimony to a rich and rewarding collaboration.

Lucy Hamilton,
Cambridge.

"مقتطفات من نشيد أوروك" التي ترجمتها جني لويس وربى أبو غيدا، للشاعر عدنان الصائغ، هي نصوصٌ مرموقةٌ بامتيازٍ. يستحضرُني هنا ما كتبه جيرمي برين في رسالتِهِ المنشورةِ إلى آندرو جورج فيما يخصُّ ترجمةَ الأخير لملحمةِ گلگامش الصادرة عن دار "بنغوين". والتي هنّأهُ فيها لقدرتِهِ على تقديمِ نصٍّ على قدرٍ كبيرٍ من الجلاءِ والقوة.. قصيدةٌ كانتْ تحملُ الكثيرَ من النبلِ والمشاعرِ، ارتبطتْ بوضوحٍ عبرَ أواصرِ عديدةٍ، امتدتْ الى البناءِ الاجتماعي للحكمِ والمغامرةِ، بين أولئكَ الرجالِ الذين كانوا ينظرون إلى ذواتِهِم بأنَّها قريبةٌ إلى عوالمِ الآلهةِ ومصادرِ القوى الخارقةِ. مع ذلك فإنَّها قوى عميقةٌ تعكسُ الرؤيةَ النفسيةَ ودواخلَ الشخصيةِ الإنسانيةِ فضلاً عن تفاعلاتِها. ولنستمعَ لعدنان الصائغ وهو يُفضي إلينا بشعرِهِ، مما نشره في حفل مجلة Long Poem، فحالما شرعَ في إلقائِهِ، انتابنا الهدوءُ للحظةٍ، ومن ثمَّ علِقنا في شبكةٍ متداخلةٍ من الحكايا.

إيان برنتون،

مجلة "Tears in the Fence" – 2015.

عن "نشيد أوروك" - الطبعة العربية الثانية 2006 والثالثة 2017

إنَّها قصيدةُ الفاجعةِ الجماعيةِ في العراق. ضحايا ينشدون نشيدَهم جماعياً أمامَ مرايا ملطّخةٍ بالدم. إنَّها قصيدةُ الكورال. تدفّقٌ لغويُّ، لغةٌ متلاطمةُ الكلماتِ والصورِ على الدوام. كما وأنَّ الشِعرَ هنا يشبهُ سدّاً في بعضِ الصفحاتِ إذ يخزنُ الماءَ بهدوءٍ ومن ثمَّ تُفتحُ البوَّاباتُ لكي تتدفقَ خارجاً وبقوةِ ألف حصانٍ شعريٍّ!

شيركو بيكه س (1940-2013)،

شاعر ومناضل كردي.

202

'Extracts from *Uruk's Anthem'* by Adnan Al-Sayegh, translated by Jenny Lewis and Ruba Abughaida, are simply outstanding. I am reminded here of the published letter of Jeremy Prynne to Andrew George concerning the latter's Penguin translation of the *Epic of Gilgamesh* in which he congratulated the translator on his ability to present 'with great clarity and force…a poem of tremendous nobility and passion, evidently linked by many threads to the social structures of governance and adventure among men who still felt themselves close to the world of an elaborate pantheon of gods and supernatural agencies, but also displaying deep powers of psychological insight and human character and interaction'. To listen to Adnan Al-Sayegh reading from his contribution to *Long Poem Magazine* at the launch was to be stilled for a moment, to be caught in a web of interwoven histories.

Ian Brinton,

Tears in the Fence, 2015

Of *Uruk's Anthem* – Arabic 2nd edition 2006 and 3rd edition 2017

It's Iraq's collective catastrophe poem. Victims collectively sing their anthem in front of blood-stained mirrors. It's a choir poem, a linguistic flux, a continuous surging of language between words and images. Also, the poetry here looks similar to a dam on some pages, as it stores the water quietly, and then the gates are opened so that it can flow out with the force of a thousand horsepower!

Sherko Bekas (1940–2013),

Kurdish poet and freedom fighter.

عن هذه الطبعة الانكليزية الجديدة

العديدُ من القرّاءِ انتظروا مختاراتٍ شاملةً من نشيد أوروك ومع هذا العرضِ اللذيذِ والمتّقدِ لـ جني لويس وربى أبوغيدا وآخرين، لدينا نصٌّ ينصفُ الأصلَ. إنَّ هذا الحضورَ المُميَّزَ لعملِ عدنان الصائغ في الأدبِ العربيِّ وكتابةِ الحربِ، يمكنُ الآن أنْ يحظى بتقديرٍ أكبر من لَدُنِ قرّاءِ اللغةِ الإنجليزية، الذين سيواجهون نصًّا مذهلاً ممتزجاً، يصهرُ التقاليدَ العربيةَ والأوروبيةَ معاً. نشيدُ أوروك؛ خيالٌ ملحميٌّ، بيدَ أنَّهُ حقيقيٌّ لا لبسَ فيه، ومرعبٌ غالباً، من قِبلِ راوٍ كان شاهداً على وقائعَ مهشمةٍ ومشاركاً فعّالاً أيضاً كان يحاولُ إيجادَ منطقٍ في عالمٍ فوضويٍّ، حيثُ القصيدةُ هي المكانُ الوحيدُ الذي يمكنُ أنْ يكون فيه المنفى وطناً. في ثنايا الكتابِ هناك أناسٌ عاديون؛ يحبُّونَ، يتوقونَ، يضحكونَ، يقنطونَ. لكنَّهم في قبضةِ قوىً كبيرةٍ ضاغطةٍ: سياسيةٍ وتاريخيةٍ وكونيةٍ. وعلى الرغمِ من ذلك كلِّهِ، فأنَّ هذا العملَ الضخمَ للصائغ يأبى أنْ يستكينَ، متمسِّكاً بقوةِ ايمانِهِ في قدرةِ الشعرِ على التفكُّرِ والخلاص.

نيال مونرو،
مدير مركز أكسفورد بروكس للشعر.

قصيدة رائعة، في ذاتِ الوقت سرمدية وموضوعية. وبينهما، قدَّمتْ لنا جني لويس وروبى أبو غيدا، ترجمةً حيَّةً سلسةً، بشعريةٍ تليقُ بهذا العملِ الهام.

جيم بوستر.

لأنْ أرى مثلَ هذه الاختياراتِ المهمةِ، لهذا العملِ الكبيرِ من الأدبِ العالمي، خلال هذه الترجمة النابضة، يمنحني سعادةً طاغيةً. هذا الشاعرُ المرهفُ إزَاءَ الهَلعِ والحُنُوِّ، وقد وجدَ المترجمين الذين يستحقهم.

ليونا مدلين.

204

Of this new English edition

Many readers have awaited an extensive selection from *Uruk's Anthem*, and in this sympathetic and acute rendering by Jenny Lewis, Ruba Abughaida and others, we have a version that does justice to the original. Already a significant presence in Arabic literature and war writing, Adnan Al-Sayegh's work can now be more fully appreciated by English language readers, who will encounter a stunning hybrid text that fuses together Arabic and European traditions. An epic phantasmagoria, *Uruk's Anthem* is nevertheless unmistakably, often terrifyingly, real, with the speaker both a witness to shattering events and also an active participant in trying to make sense of a world in chaos where the poem is the only place where the exile can be at home. At the heart of the book are ordinary people who love, lust, laugh and despair, but are in the grip of vast political, historical, and cosmic forces. And yet despite it all, Al-Sayegh's monumental work refuses to submit, holding fervently to a belief in the power of poetry to reckon and redeem.

Niall Munro,

Director, Oxford Brookes Poetry Centre.

A remarkable poem, at once timeless and topical. Between them, Jenny Lewis and Ruba Abughaida have produced a lively, fluent and appropriately poetic translation of this important work.

Jem Poster.

To see such a significant selection from this major work of world literature in this thrilling translation gives me great pleasure. This fine poet of terror and tenderness has found the translators he deserves.

Leona Medlin.

هوامش المقدمة

[1] في البعضِ من البلدان العربية، تمَّ حَظرُ "نشيد أوروك"، أو حَذفُ أقسام منه.

[2] بعد اخراج مقتطفات من "نشيد أوروك" في عملٍ مسرحي (قُدم العرض الأول عام 1989. والثاني منه عام 1993 على خشبةِ مسرح الرشيد في بغداد)، وقدْ لاقى حينها استحساناً واسعاً، لكنه أغضبَ السلطة، مما اضطرَ الصائغ لمغادرةِ العراق في العام نفسه 1993. وبعد صدورِ طبعةٍ نشيد أوروك في بيروت عام 1996 وجدَ الصائغ اسمَهُ على رأسِ "قائمة الموتِ" التي أصدرها عدي نجل صدام حسين. وبعد التغيرات التي جرثْ في العراق، وإبّان دعوته للمشاركة في مهرجان المربد الشعري، في مدينة البصرة عام 2006، أزعجتْ قصائدُهُ أيضاً الميليشياتِ المسلّحةَ المتعصبةَ دينياً، فتعرّض مجدداً للتهديدات بقطع لسانه وبالموت. وعلى إثرها غادرَ البصرة مضطراً، عابراً إلى الكويت ومنها عائداً إلى منفاه في لندن.

[3] "المعلقات" او ما تسمى بـ"القصائد المعلّقة"– هي عبارة عن سبع قصائد عربية طويلة، تم تعليقها على جدرانِ الكعبة (قبل الإسلام).

[4] الاسم الأدبي للدبلوماسي والكاتب الفرنسي أليكسيس ليجيه 1975–1887.

[5] من قصيدة "أريدكِ" للشاعر عدنان الصائغ، "غناء لـ اينانا"، دار نشر مولفران 2014.

[6] البروفيسور هناء خليّف غني: "ما بين الوطن والمنفى: قراءة في تجربة المنفى للشاعر العراقي عدنان الصائغ"؛ قدمتها إلى قسم الترجمة – الجامعة المستنصرية/ العراق. ونشرتها في مجلة التقدم في اللغة والدراسات، إصدار 4717– 2203 ، رقم المجلد 3، حزيران 2016، المركز الأسترالي الأكاديمي – أستراليا.

[7] "أوراق من سيرة تأبط منفى"، منشورات ARC صدرثْ عام 2016، ترجمة: ستيفن واتس، ومارغا بورغي– آرتاخو، ص 35.

[8] يانيس ريتسوس، شاعر يوناني وناشط، 1990–1909. صاحب القصيدة التاريخية "الرثاء"، والتي تمثل منارةً في الشعر، نُثِرتْ عام 1936، وكانت عبارة عن رسالة تدعو لوحدة جميع الناس. لكن في وقتٍ لاحق من ذلك العام كانت قد وصلتْ ديكتاتورية أيوانيس متاكساس اليمينية إلى السلطة، وقامت بحرق قصيدة "الرثاء" علانيّةً عند سفح جبل أثينا.

[9] يعدُّ منجزُ الصائغ الشعري هذا موضوعاً معتَمداً في بعض الأطاريح في بلده العراق وفي الشتات الأوسع. إحدى الدراساتِ التي شعر بها بشكلٍ خاص تقترّب من فهم طبيعة كتابته لشعر الحرب، هي مقارنةٌ لقصائد حرب مختارة لـ"ويلفرد أوين" و "عدنان الصائغ" – دراسة نفسية قدمتها سرى حسين محمد علي. ونالتْ بها درجة الماجستير في الآداب، من قبل كلية التربية للبنات – قسم اللغة الإنجليزية، جامعة بغداد، 2014.

[10] هذا المقطع لـ ويلفرد أوين، شأنه شأن جميع مقتطفات قصائده المذكورة ضمن هذه المقدمة، قام بتحريرها كل من: جون ستالوورثي، جاتو، و ويندساس. ص 143.

[11] مقدّمةعن قصيدة "بين قوسين" طبعة فاير وفاير، 1937. نُثِرثْ هذه الطبعة عام 2010. ص 13.

[12] "هل تسمعين حفيفَ الغصونِ التي تتساقطُ..

هل تسمعين رفيفَ البراعمِ تُزهرُ...

هل تسمعين... ني ني ني ني ني ني

بأفواههم" – من "نشيد أوروك" ص 40

[13] مقدّمة عن قصيدة "بين قوسين" طبعة فاير وفاير، 1937. ص 12.

[14] المرجعُ السابق، ص 11.

206

Notes on Introduction

1 *Uruk's Anthem* is banned or only available in expurgated editions in many Arab countries.

2 Al-Sayegh was forced to flee from Iraq in 1993 after extracts from his work were adapted for the stage and first performed, in 1989 and then in 1993, at the Rasheed Theatre in Baghdad where the play received wide acclaim but also angered the government. After the publication of *Uruk's Anthem* in Beirut in 1996, Al-Sayegh found that his name was top of Saddam Hussein's son Uday's death list. Even after the changes that took place in Iraq, when he read in Basra at the Al-Marbed Poetry Festival in 2006, the poems upset the intolerant religious armed militia and Al-Sayegh was again threatened with death and with having his tongue cut out. He was forced to leave Basra in haste and fled through Kuwait to return to his exile in London.

3 The Mu'allaqāt, or 'Hanging Poems' is a group of seven long Arabic poems that were hung on or in the Kaaba at Mecca.

4 The pseudonym of the French diplomat and writer, Alexis Leger, 1887–1975.

5 From 'I Need You' by Adnan Al-Sayegh, *Singing for Inanna*, Mulfran Press, 2014.

6 Professor Hana Khliaf Ghena, Between Home and Exile: A Reading of the Exilic Experience of the Iraqi Poet Adnan Al-Sayegh, Advances in Language and Literary Studies, Department of Translation. Al-Mustansiriyah University, Iraq; published in *Language and Literary Studies*, ISSN: 2203–4714 Vol. No 3; June 2016, Australian Academic Centre, Australia.

7 From *Pages from the Biography of an Exile*, ARC Publications 2016, translated by Stephen Watts and Marga Burgui-Artajo, p.35.

8 Yannis Ritsos, Greek poet and activist, 1909–1990. His landmark poem *Epitaphios*, published in 1936, expressed a message of the unity of all people, but later that year the right-wing dictatorship of Ioannis Metaxas came to power and *Epitaphios* was burned publicly at the foot of the Acropolis in Athens.

9 Al-Sayegh's work is a popular subject for theses in Iraq and the wider diaspora. One which he felt particularly grasped the nature of his work as a 'war poet' was a MA thesis – A Comparative Study of Selected War Poems by Wilfred Owen and Adnan Al-Sayegh; A Psychological Study, submitted by Sura-Hussein-Mohammed Ali. It was awarded a degree by the College of Education for Women, The Department of English, The University of Baghdad, 2014.

10 This, as with all extracts of Owen's poems cited in this introduction, is from *The Poems of Wilfred Owen*, edited by Jon Stallworthy, Chatto and Windus, p.143.

11 Preface to *In Parenthesis*, Faber and Faber, 1937, this edition published 2010, p. xiii.

12 'Do you hear the falling branches whispering?
Do you hear the budding buds shimmering?
Do you hear me me me me me me me
                   in their mouths,' *Uruk's Anthem*, p. 40.

13 Preface to *In Parenthesis*, Faber and Faber, 1937, p. xii.

14 Ibid, p. xi.

هوامش نشيد اوروك

15 خوفو: من الفراعنة المصريين يعودُ اليه بناء الهرم الأكبر في الجيزة.

16 المعرّي (973–1057م): فيلسوف وشاعر وكاتب عربي أعمى.

17 نيبور: أول مدينة على الأرض في الأساطير السومرية.

18 إشارة إلى عين الشمس لقب لـ "النظام" الفتاة التي أحبّها محي الدين بن عربي (1165–1240) وكتب من أجلها ديوان شعره "ترجمان الاشواق".

19 ننماخ: "السيدة العظيمة"، إلهة بابلية مهمة.

20 مردوخ: الإله البابلي الأساسي.

21 اللازورد: العَوْهَق [في لسان العرب والقاموس المحيط].

22 استفادة من الشاعر السريالي اندريه بريتون في وصف صديقه الشاعر دسنوس: "إنه يقرأُ في نفسه كما في كتاب مفتوح ولا يفعلُ شيئاً لحفظ الأوراقِ التي تتطايرُ في رياحِ حياتِه".

23 آنونّي: من نَسل إله السماء آن وقرينته إلهة الأرض كاي.

24 ايكيكي: مجمع آلهة الأرض السومرية ويضمُّ 50 إلهاً صغيراً.

25 عام المجاعة الكبرى؛ ألغى خلالها الخليفةُ الحاكمُ [عمر بن الخطّاب]، عقوبةَ السرقة.

26 كان عمر بن عبيد (توفي 761) أحدُ قادةِ الحركة اللاهوتية "العقلانية" لدى المعتزلة. حين مرَّ بجماعة وقوف، فقال: ما هذا؟ قيل: السلطانُ يقطعُ يَدَ سارقٍ. فقال: لا إله إلّا الله سارقُ العلانيةِ يقطعُ سارقَ السرِّ.

27 شعلان أبو الجون، أحدُ أبطال ثورة العشرين.

28 سورةُ الفتح: آية قرآنية.

29 عشتار: إلهةُ الحبِّ والجنسِ والجاذبيةِ والخصوبةِ والحرب والقتالِ والسلطةِ السياسيةِ في بلاد ما بين النهرين.

30 إشارة إلى عنوان كتاب لناظم حكمت.

31 إشارة إلى الشاعر الجاهلي تأبَّطَ شراً، المتوفى سنة 540 م.

32 إشارة الى النبيِّ محمد.

33 إشارة إلى لقاء للشاعر الفرزدق مع الحسين بن علي (626–680).

34 إشارة إلى رقيب فرنسيٍّ عام 1915، عندما هاجمه الألمان في خندقٍ وكان جميعُ رفاقِهِ موتى فصاح: "قياماً أيها الموتى".

35 اهزوجة تحريضية لأحد أبناء الريف، طعنَ بفالتِهِ جندياً بريطانياً، ويطالبه أن يُعيدها إليه قائلاً: [مشكول الذمة على الفالة]!..

36 وحدةٌ زمنيةٌ في أحد التقاويم الهندوسية حيثُ اليومُ والليلةُ من البراهما يساوي ملايينَ السنين البشرية.

37 الشلمغاني: كاتب ولاهوتي مسلم عُرف بكتبه في الفقهِ وموضوعاتٍ أخرى. وقد أُعدمَ بتهمةِ الهرطقة عام 934 م وأحرق جسدُه.

38 تيامت هي الإلهة الأساس للبحر المالح والتي تزاوجتْ مع أبسو إله المياه العذبة، لصنعِ الآلهةِ الأصغرِ سناً. إوهي ترمزُ إلى هيولى الخلق.

39 مامو أو مامي: إلهةٌ في الملحمة البابلية " أترا حاسيس"، وفي أساطير الخلق الأخرى التي خلقت البشر من الدم والطين.

40 لخمو و لخامو: أول إلهين ولدا من الطمي (أو الحطام) وقد نشأا من خلال التحام تيامِت وأبسو.

41 أنشار وكيشار: إلهان توأم يمثلان أفقيْ السماء والأرض.

42 آنو: إلهُ سماء ميزوبوتاميا. كاي: إلهةُ الأرض. آيا[كان إلها ذكراً ثمَّ]:إلهة الفجر وعروس شماش إله الشمس.

43 استفادة قرآنية.

44 كاظم عبد، سيد حرز[مصاب بالشيزوفرنيا]، قاسم مشعان، علي ناصر، مكي دفّار، حسن صكبان، فاضل جمعة، أبو شكر الحلاق، وجنود آخرون، شاركوا الصانع أقسى الأيّام، في المعسكرات والخنادق المختلفة، خلال سنوات الحرب العراقية الإيرانية الطويلة الطاحنة.

45 إشارة إلى القصائد المتهكِّمة والمتمردة لابن اللنكك البصري (توفي 970 م).

46 من كلام أخوان الصفا وخُلّان الوفا.

Notes on *Uruk's Anthem*

[15] Khofu: an Egyptian pharaoh credited with having commissioned the Great Pyramid of Giza.

[16] Al-Muari (973–1057 AD): a blind Arab philosopher, poet and writer.

[17] Naybur: the first city on earth, according to Sumerian mythology.

[18] A reference to 'Ain Shams', an epithet for Al-Nedam, the girl whom Ibn 'Arabi (1165–1240) loved and for whom he wrote the book *Translation of Longings*.

[19] Nanmakh: the 'Great Lady', an important Babylonian goddess.

[20] Marduk: the primary Babylonian god.

[21] Lapis lazuli.

[22] The Surrealist poet André Breton said of his friend Robert Desnos 'He reads himself like an open book and does nothing to stop its pages flying in the winds of his life.'

[23] Annunaki: offspring of the sky god An and his consort, the earth goddess, Kai.

[24] Ikeeki: a compound of the Sumerian Earth Goddess comprising fifty minor deities.

[25] The year of the Great Famine during which the ruling Caliph [Umar ibn Al-Khattab] abolished the punishment for stealing.

[26] Omar Bin Ubayd (died 761) was one of the earliest leaders of the 'rationalist' theological movement of the Mu'tazili. Passing a group of onlookers he asked what was going on and they told him 'The sultan is cutting off the hand of a thief...' to which he replied 'The thief who steals in public is cutting off the hand of the thief who steals in private!'

[27] Sha'lan Abdul-Jun: one of the heroes of the post-1920 revolution in Iraq.

[28] Surat Al-Fath: a verse from the Qur'an.

[29] Ishtar: Mesopotamian goddess of love, sex, desire, fertility, war, combat and political power.

[30] A reference to the title of a book by Nazim Hikmet.

[31] A reference to the pre-Islamic poet Ta'Aebbata Sharran who died in 540 AD.

[32] A reference to the prophet Mohammed.

[33] A reference to a meeting by the poet Al-Farazdaq and Al-Hussein Bin Ali (626–680).

[34] A reference to a French sergeant in 1915, the last man standing of his battalion, who, when attacked by the Germans shouted to the dead 'Arise, my friends!'

[35] From a revolutionary song in which a peasant, after stabbing a British soldier with his pitchfork, asks politely for his pitchfork back.

[36] A unit of time in one of the Hindu calendars in which a day and night of the Brahma eqates to millions of human years.

[37] Al-Shalmaghani: a Muslim writer, best known for his books on jurisprudence and other subjects. He was executed for heresy in 934 AD and his body was burned.

[38] Tiamat: the primordial goddess of the salt sea who mates with Abzû, the god of fresh water, to produce younger deities. She symbolises the chaos of creation.

[39] Mamu or Mami: a goddess in the Babylonian epic Atra-Hasis and other creation legends who created humans from blood and clay.

[40] Lahmu and Lahamu: the first gods to be born from the silt (or debris) created by the merging of Tiamat and Abzû.

[41] Anshar and Kishar: twin gods representing the horizons of sky and earth.

[42] Anu: the Mesopotamian sky god; Kai, an earth goddess; Aya, goddess of dawn, bride of Shamash the sun god.

[43] Qur'an usage.

[44] Kadhim Abed: along with Sayid Herez (a schizophrenic), Qasim Meshan, Ali Naser, Makki Daffar, Hasan Sagban, Fadhil Jumeah, Bu Shokr Al-Halaq and all the other soldiers who shared the toughest days with Al-Sayegh, in various camps and trenches, during the long, cruel years of the Iran–Iraq War.

[45] Reference to the satirical, insurgent poems of Ibn Al-Lankik Al-Basri (970 AD).

[46] From the sayings of Akhwan Al-Safda and Khala Al-Wafa.

47 مثل شعبي: "راح النهار بنفخة نار".

48 الأصمعي (740–828م) مُشبِّهاً تسارعَ العمر برجلٍ رآه على جسرٍ ببغداد يبيعُ الثلجَ في عزِّ الصيفِ وهو يصيحُ بالمارة: ارحموا رجلاً رأسماله يذوب.

49 من أغاني الطفولة.

50 المرجع السابق.

51 تحوير لقصيدة القيرواني: "يا ليلُ، الصبُّ متى غدهُ / أقيام الساعةِ موعدُهُ".

52 إشارة إلى بيتٍ للشاعر كزار حنتوش.

53 أحدُ بحور الشعر العربيِّ، يطلق عليه "الخَبَب" تشبيها له بجري الخيل. تتبدل فيه الوحدات الايقاعية، طولاً وقصراً. ويسمى أيضاً المُتَدَارَكُ، أو المُحْدَثُ..

54 محمد الگبنجي مطرب عراقي قديم من بغداد.

55 الخيزاران (توفت عام 789م) كانت جارية تزوجت الخليفة/المهدي/ وأصبحت ذات سلطة قوية – كانت ثروتها تقدر بـ 160 مليون درهم. وعندما أغضبها ابنُها/الخليفة/موسى الهادي، حقدتْ عليه وأمرت الجواري بالجلوس على وجهه حتى خنقنه.

56 في إشارة الى جارية تكنى بأم موسى أمرتها مولاتها شغب وهي والدة الخليفة[المقتدر بالله] أن تجلس في مجلس القضاء للمظالم. فأخذت تصدر أوامر المصادرات. وشغب كانت متلهفةً للمال جمعت ما في خزائن الخلافة من العنبر والمسك لتصنع حوضاً لتغمس به هي وجواريها أقدامَهُنَّ.

57 إشارة إلى بيت أبي نؤاس (756–814م):"ما لي وللناس كم يلحونني سفهاً/ ديني لنفسي ودينُ الناس للناس".

58 إقتباس من الشاعر الفرنسي سان جون بيرس.

59 إقتباس من مهربان خاتون (1858 – 1905) شاعرة كردية. وكانت جميلة طلب أميرٌ يدها للزواج، ولكنه حين سمع قصيدتها هذه التي صورتْ فيها حبها لابن عمها: "لقد أضحى قلبي قطعاً متناثرةً وروحي شعلة من اللهب الذائب" (وتخلصُ القصيدةُ إلى أنه إذا كان هناك شغفٌ بين قلبين فلا يمكن فصلهما)، فتراجع الأميرُ عن الزواج.

60 اقتباس من الشاعر رشدي العامل: "أرجوكم لا تضعوا المرايا في قبري، ولا الكتبَ ولا الأوراقَ تحتَ رأسي، فأنا تعبٌ أريدُ أنْ أذوقَ طعمَ النوم".

61 إقتباس من عبد القادر الجناني: "البراكينُ زفيرُ الطبيعة".

62 إقتباس من معين بسيسو: "القاتلُ واضحٌ والضحيةُ واضحةٌ فلماذا الغموض".

63 إقتباس من الشاعر عقيل علي في "طائر آخر يتوارى".

64 ماعت: إلهة الصدق والعدالة والنظام الكوني عند المصريين القدماء، ولعدالتها استخدمتْ ريشتها لوزنِ روح الميت، وكان ذلكَ شعارُها.

65 إلتجرا ؛ في الأساطير الأوقيانوسية ، تشهدُ له قبائل أراندا في وسط أستراليا باعتباره والد السماء المسؤول عن وقتِ الأحلام.

66 جوجوليان؛ بطل ومحارب ايرلندي شبه أسطوري. عندما حاصر قلعة أميان خرجتْ مائةُ امرأةٍ عاريةٍ رمين عليه ماءً بارداً ومغلياً حتى استسلم.

67 قدموس؛ مؤسس مدينة طيبة وأول ملوكها، في الأساطير اليونانية.

68 طاغية روماني، وضعتْ عشيقتُهُ له السمَّ.

69 طاغية روماني، قطَّعت أوصاله الجماهير عام 222م.

70 طاغية روماني آخر، قتلته الجماهير وحملوا رأسَهُ ورؤوسَ وزرائِهِ على رماحِهم. علَّق أحدُ المؤرخين: "إنَّ الطغاةَ لا يموتون في أسرَّتِهم".

71 إمبراطور صيني (1360 –1424) حكم على كاتب بالإعدامِ، وقبل أنْ يلفظَ ذلك الكاتبُ أنفاسَهُ الأخيرةَ استطاعَ أنْ يكتبَ كلمةً واحدةً ضدَّهُ: "خائن".

72 "الجميع يقول: نعم سيدي"، من قصيدة للشاعر أونيسيمو سيلفيرا؛ سياسي وكاتب، من جزر الرأس الأخضر. ولد عام 1935، قضى 3 سنوات محكوماً بالأشغال الشاقة.

73 إشارة إلى رسالة حمزة بن علي إلى الخليفة الحاكم بأمر الله (386 – 411 هـ).

74 إشارة إلى انتفاضةِ الشعب المنغولي عام 1961 والتي سقط فيها ما يزيد عن 50 ألف قتيل.

75 إشارة إلى قصيدة للشاعر الأعمى بشار بن برد (714–784م).

76 إشارة إلى الوضع المأساوي في كربلاء عقب انتفاضة آذار 1991.

[47] An old saying: 'Time has vanished like a puff of fire.'

[48] Al-Asmaei (740–828) compared life to a man selling ice on a Baghdad bridge in the heat of summer, shouting at passers-by 'Have mercy on a man whose capital is melting!'

[49] From an old children's song.

[50] Ibid.

[51] A reference to the poet Al-Qayrawani's line 'O night, when morning comes, will it be judgement day?'

[52] A line in a poem by Kzar Hantosh.

[53] A type of prosody which alternates groups of long and short syllables in a specific way. Also known as Khabab (الخبب) 'ambling' or Muḥdath (المحدث) 'innovative'.

[54] Mohammed Al-Gubunchi, an old Iraqi singer from Baghdad.

[55] Al-Khaizaran (died 789) was a slave girl who married the Caliph and became very powerful – she was worth 160 million dirham. When her son, Musa Al-Hadi, angered her she ordered his concubines to sit on his face and suffocate him.

[56] Referring to a maid, nicknamed Om Musa, who was appointed by her mistress Shaghab, mother of the Caliph, to run a court hearing about the confiscation of goods. However, Shaghab herself was guilty of appropriating state funds to have a pool built of amber and musk for her and her ladies to plunge their feet into.

[57] A reference to the poet Abu Nawwas (756–814) who asked 'Why do I care about those who revile me for extravagance?/ My religion is only mine and theirs is only theirs.'

[58] Quotation from the French poet, Saint-John Perse.

[59] Quotation from Mahrabban Khatton (1858–1905), a Kurdish poet. In his poem, a prince proposes to a beautiful woman, but he reads a poem she has written to her cousin with whom she is in love – 'My heart has become scattered in pieces / And my soul is a flame of melted fire.' The poem concludes that if there is passion between two hearts 'they cannot be separated.' So the prince withdraws his offer of marriage.

[60] Quotation from a poem by Rushdi Al-Amil: 'Do not put mirrors in my grave, nor books nor papers under my head. I'm tired and I want to sleep.'

[61] Quotation from Abdulqader Al-Janabi: 'Volcanoes are nature's exhalations.'

[62] Quotation from Moein Bassiso: 'The killer is clear and the victim is clear. Why the mystery?'

[63] Quotation from Aqeel Ali: 'Another bird is fading away.'

[64] Maat: the ancient Egyptian personification of truth, justice and the cosmic order. She weighed the heart of the deceased against an ostrich feather which was her emblem.

[65] Altjira, in Oceanian mythology, is recognised by the Aranda tribes in Central Australia as the sky father responsible for dreamtime.

[66] Cú Chulainn: an Irish semi-mythical hero and warrior. When he besieged the castle of Amian a hundred naked women came out and poured hot and cold water on him until he surrendered.

[67] Cadmus was the founder and first king of Thebes in Greek mythology.

[68] A Roman tyrant poisoned by his mistress.

[69] A Roman tyrant cut to pieces by the mob in 222 AD.

[70] Another Roman tyrant. The mob killed him and paraded his head, with the heads of his ministers, on their spears. As a historian once remarked – 'Tyrants rarely die in their beds.'

[71] A Chinese Emperor (1360–1424) who sentenced a writer to death but not before the writer had managed to write one word against him: 'Traitor'.

[72] 'Everybody says 'Yes Sir!': from a poem by Onésimo Silveira, a Cape Verdean politician and writer born in 1935 who was sentenced to three years hard labour.

[73] A reference to a letter from Hamza Bin Ali to the Caliph Al-Hakim Bi Amrillah (386–411 AD).

[74] A reference to the Mongolian uprising of 1961 which resulted in 50,000 deaths.

[75] A reference to a poem by the blind poet Bashar ibn Burd (714–784).

[76] A reference to the tragic situation in Karbala after the uprising in March 1991.

⁷⁷ إشارة إلى كأس كورماك كوبلينان، الملك والاسقف والحكيم الايرلندي في القرن التاسع.
وهي كأسٌ إذا قِيلتْ أمامَها ثلاث أكاذيب تتكسّر إلى ثلاثِ قطع وإذا قيلتْ أمامَها ثلاث حقائق تعودُ إلى ما كانتْ عليه.

⁷⁸ إشارة إلى النائمين السبعة، في كلٍّ من التقاليد المسيحية والإسلامية، الذين اختبأوا داخلَ كهفٍ خارج مدينة أفسس حوالي 250 قبل الميلاد هرباً من الاضطهاد الديني، وظهروا بعد حوالي 300 سنة.

⁷⁹ إشارة إلى الأقدار الثلاثة.

⁸⁰ أميليو برادوسن: "أسير في إثرِك خطوةً خطوةً ألا ترى ذلك؟ فأنني أضيعُ خطوةً خطوةً".

⁸¹ إقتباس من "بحيرة الجزيرة" لأزرا باوند: "رباه، فينوس، ميركور يا شفيع اللصوص / امنحوني دُكّان تبغ صغيرة/ أو أعينوني في أية حرفة/ عدا هذه الحرفة اللعينة، حرفة الكتابة".

⁸² رثاء ننكال من كتاب سفر سومر: "ويحك يا نِنار لقد هوثْ مقدساتُ أور وذبحَ البرابرةُ شعبَك ويحي يا نِنار لا معبدَ لك ولي، ولا مدينة لك ولي، لقد تشرّدَ القومُ واصبحتْ أورُ خراباً".

⁸³ إشارة إلى أولِ سطرٍ في ملحمة كلكامش: "هو الذي رأى كلَّ شيءٍ".

⁸⁴ الحسين بن علي بن أبي طالب ويزيد بن معاوية انغمسا في نزاعاتٍ في أوائل الخلافة الأموية، انتهت بمقتل الحسين.

⁸⁵ القَطَا: طائر يأكلُ البذورَ ويوجدُ في الصحارى والأماكنِ الجافةِ في العالمِ.

⁸⁶ دلمون (تلمون)؛ الفردوس السومري، وأرض الطهارة والخلود.

[77] A reference to the grail of Cormac Cuilennáin, the ninth century Irish king, bishop and sage. If three lies are told before the grail, it will break into three pieces. If three truths are said before it, it will return to its original condition.

[78] A reference to the Seven Sleepers, from both Christian and Islamic traditions, who hid inside a cave outside the city of Ephesus around 250 BC to escape religious persecution, and emerged some 300 years later.

[79] A reference to the three Fates.

[80] Emilio Baradson: 'I follow behind you, step by step, don't you see that? And step by step, I get lost.'

[81] Reference to 'The Lake Isle', by Ezra Pound: 'O God, O Venus, O Mercury, patron of thieves,/ Lend me a little tobacco-shop,/ Or install me in any profession / Save this damn'd profession of writing...'

[82] Ninkal's Lament is from the Book of Sumer: 'Oh city lament.../ Your sacred temples have been destroyed and your gardens are ruined.../ The barbarians have slaughtered your people.../ Your people have been exiled and Ur is destroyed...'

[83] A reference to the Prologue to the *Epic of Gilgamesh* which begins 'He Who Saw Everything' (translated into Arabic by Taha Baqir, Baghdad, 1962); or 'He Who Saw the Deep' (translated into English by Andrew George, London, 1999).

[84] Al-Ḥusayn ibn Ali ibn Abi Talib and Yazīd ibn Mu'āwiya indulged in quarrels in the early Umayyad caliphate, it ended with the killing of Hussein.

[85] Sandgrouse: a seed eating bird found in the deserts and dry places of the world.

[86] Dilmun (Telmun) was a Sumerian paradise and the land of purity and eternity.